Special Occasion Helps

C.M. O'Guin

PULPIT LIBRARY

AKER BOOK HOUSE Grand Rapids, Michigan 49506

ISBN: 0-8010-6650-6

Library of Congress Catalog Card Number: 65-18265

Fifth printing, January 1990

Printed in the United States of America

CONTENTS

Introduction

Part I. Helps for Special Occasions

Part II. Helps for Special Days

PREFACE

We turn over to you, my fellow ministers, *Special Occasion Helps,* gauged to relieve part of your heavy work-load. The author, being a member of your craft, was privileged to sit at the feet of men blessed with bounteous gifts and superbly equipped for the ministry, and they shared with him their gleanings from the Lord's Vineyard. These Gamaliels of the ministry (Acts 22:3) pass on these suggestions to those of you who are on the firing line and know the heat and force of the Gospel battle. In placing this type of book in your hands, it is not our purpose to set aside your own thinking machinery with which God has endowed all His servants, but to give you a source of inspiration when you are empty, dry and stale.

The plan we followed incorporates into one book a broad scope of messages formerly found only by looking from book to book. This feature of convenience will be appreciated by the users. Funeral messages with substantial invocation, sermon and ritual at the grave; ordination to the ministry with vows and charges; dedicatory messages for churches with delivery of key and full length ceremony; baccalaureate sermons for both high schools and colleges; and marriage ceremonies and golden wedding anniversaries have not, in the past, been found in the same volume.

As a busy pastor, with a heavy schedule of activities outside the church, I well know the *river* from the minister's preaching well dwindles at times to a mere trickle, and his preaching dynamo ceases to hum, squeaks and cries for fresh oil, and at times his preaching oven is not baking the bread thoroughly and the output shrinks to a dry crust, then he needs stimulation. Samson found it after crying "I thirst" and turned aside and drank from the hollow of a mule's jaw and his spirit came again and he revived (Judg. 15:19). If my dedicated, toiling and burdened "yoke-fellows" in the Gospel find the least assistance here, I shall be rewarded (Phil. 4:3).

A PRAYER FOR PREACHERS

Our Father, we come to Thee in the name of Jesus, our blessed Lord.

We have prayed for help and health for others, but now we come to Thee for ourselves. We know we are not worthy that Thou shouldest come under our roof, yet we have been chosen to preach Thy Word and to administer the ordinances of Thy house. We have heard Thy voice and accepted a call to Thy ministry. Make us conscious of the responsibilities which are ours and give us strength for the obligations. Keep us from the temptations peculiar to our calling. If we have loved power and leadership more than service for Thee, rebuke us. If we have been too engrossed in little things, forgive us. If we have been more concerned with the strong and the rich than with the shepherdless throngs, open our eyes to our sins. If we have been more loyal to the church of the past than to the vision of today, help us to a new attitude.

Holy Father, we pray for humility and contrition. As we interpret Thy Word to a hungry people may we give them the bread that satisfies. Free us from the entanglements that have hushed the thundering prophetic voice. Make us brave and bold in our day of coldness and bewilderment. Give us personalities which radiate love and faith.

We know we are weak, but we pray to be saved from failure. Help us to remember we have the vows of God upon us. Our hands have gripped the gospel plow and we have gone too far to turn back.

Help us to view sin with horror but always to show compassion for the weak and frail. Teach us to love our enemies. Make us faithful shepherds of Thy flock, true seers of God, and true followers of Jesus Christ, for in His name we pray. Amen.

INTRODUCTION

THE MINISTER'S MESSAGE

"So thou, O son of man, I have set thee a watchman over the house of Israel; therefore thou shalt hear the word at my mouth, and warn them from me. . . . Say unto them; as I live, saith the Lord God" (Ezek. 33:7-11).

In Ezekiel 33, we find an excellent definition of true preaching. The preacher is simply the mouthpiece of Almighty God. He can only impart to the people that which he received from the Lord. And what is the source of his knowledge? The eternal Word of God! True preaching would therefore be Word-preaching, or Bible preaching—declaration and application of Holy Writ.

For the true believer, the pulpit is the place from which the New Testament prophet speaks under the anointing of the Holy Ghost, with the greatest conviction and power ever in the spirit of, "Thus saith the Lord."

There should never be any doubt in the mind and heart of the preacher that he addresses the church and the work in the NAME (or in the stead) of the Lord. He dare not enter the pulpit if he entertains any doubt in his heart as to this. The church is waiting for a message from the Lord, not for sentiment and opinions of man. The preacher should also be conscious of what God expects him to convey to His church. He is truly an ambassador of heaven (2 Cor. 5:20).

The consciousness of this single honor should call for humility and careful behaviour. There can be no question of conceit. Rather let it be a divine dignity covered in true humility. In spite of his unworthiness and inability, God thought it good in infinite grace to call man as His mouthpiece. This humility, coupled with dignity, is clearly observed in the ministry of Moses, Ezekiel, Amos, John the Baptist, the Apostle Paul and others. It is not a self assumed honor or dignity. It is divinely conferred. Therefore, the sincere preacher will always seek the mind of the Lord in order to declare with authority: "Thus saith the Lord." And if the Lord has not spoken, he will remain silent, lest he should impute to the Lord what He never said.

The entire Scriptures, both Old and New Testaments, are a revelation of God in Christ. True Word-preaching would therefore of necessity be true Christ-preaching and could never degenerate to the mere presentation of morals or the telling of sob-stories or yet, a demand for political and social reform.

Christ-centered preaching is the demand of the Word, the nourishment of the church and the need of the world! The pastor has many responsibilities, but his primary function is ever that of the preacher of the Holy Word. The history of this world records the abdication of kings for the sake of other considerations and hardly ever does it refer to such kings with respect. Unfortunately, church history also records men of God and preachers who forsook the pulpit for the sake of other considerations, and too frequently these "considerations" were material gain. Regrettable as this is, it is not as sad as men remaining in the ministry who have become unfaithful to their charge and have abused the office by becoming mere social workers, reformers, political speakers and agitators. Such men have discredited the ministry and have failed to be true mouthpieces of the Lord. They should resign their office. The minister, truly called of the Lord, cannot afford to serve two masters. One is his Master, even the Lord. Therefore, his attitude should ever be: "Lord, what wilt thou have me to do [or say]?" (Acts 9:6). A full surrender and absolute consecration to the Lord and His church is all that can meet the demands of the ministry.

The minister is in the forefront. Christ said "All power is given unto me in heaven and earth" (Matt. 28:18-19). The word "therefore" followed His assertion, "All power is given unto me." God says in effect, "You go; I have the power." God's plan from the beginning was to reach men by human agency. Man must "go" but only in the power of the Spirit. His promise is sure, "Lo, I am with you."

1. *We need a message that will bring a spiritual awakening,* a quickening of faith, devotion and vital activity. We need a mighty surge of spiritual life and zeal to penetrate our entire social system. Christ is a universal Saviour. He tasted death for every man. He is available for all and is sufficient for all. We who are saved are not to monopolize God's grace. God is saying to us, "Whom shall I send and who will go for us?" Many are saying "I cannot," while a few are saying "Here am I, send me."

2. *Men must go to the Bible for their message.* Timothy was commanded to do the work of an evangelist, and in doing it, to "preach the Word." The world needs the message that comes from God. The Word is a penetrating force and transforming power. This message was born in the agony of the cross and delivered by the power of the Holy Spirit from lips touched with a coal from God's own altar fires.

3. *The God-sent preacher is a herald.* He has no message of his own. It is God's message that he proclaims. According to the heraldic law of Bible times, if a herald added one word of his own to the king's, he was beheaded. If a law like this were enforced today, so many preachers would lose their heads they would be piled high as the Empire State Building in New York or the Pyramids of Egypt. Christ said, "Teach them all things whatsoever I have commanded you." When the preacher comes from the secret place of prayer with a message burning in him like fire, he will have results. The gospel has not only saved individuals, but it has awakened nations and transformed lives.

4. *The faithful preacher is a man of toil.* There is too much ease in Zion; men are looking for a soft, easy place. There is absolutely no power in a life of ease. In Romans 13:11, Paul says, "Knowing the time, that now it is high time to awake out of sleep." Solomon referred to "Too much folding of the hands to sleep" (Prov. 6:10). The preacher who is hunting for a life of ease is in the wrong vocation. The early church did not find it easy. All the apostles died martyrs for the faithful preaching of God's Word. Paul tells Timothy to "Endure afflictions, do the work of an evangelist" (2 Tim. 4:5). Timothy was also enjoined to endure hardness as a good soldier of Jesus Christ. No past generation has been more needy nor had a greater opportunity to hear the gospel than our own. We must bring His message urgently to all men. If we fail here we have not only lost a great opportunity which could well be the last, but we have failed God.

SIX PATHS TO POWER

The whole world today is power conscious. All kinds of means, good and bad, are being used to gain power over others. Even Christians many times fail to recognize the greatest power of all! The power and glory of God's presence is witnessed in operation among individuals and churches who follow Bible instructions. Let us mention:

1. *The Power of Repentance*. 2 Chron. 7:14 says, "If my people which are called by my name, shall humble themselves and pray, and seek my face, and turn from their wicked ways, then will I hear from heaven and will forgive their sin and will heal their land."

It is possible for Christians to trust in themselves that they are righteous and overlook the possibility of sinning and fail to repent when they are wrong. The time is upon us when we all need to repent, as individuals, churches and nations; to search ourselves and turn back to God who in turn will pour out His blessing upon us.

With the world, or Satan, making inroads into the church so rapidly, we need to repent and have a great revival. We are in need of soul-searching and soul-stirring. Men are perishing in sin and unbelief, and in order to reach them, we must repent and regain old losses and new power. Repentance is the gateway into a life of spiritual power.

2. *The Power of Prayer*. Acts 16:25: "At midnight Paul and Silas prayed and sang praises unto God." "The effectual fervent prayer of a righteous man availeth much" (James 5:16). Prayer is one of the greatest weapons a Christian has to combat evil, yet it is so greatly neglected. Prayer has turned the tide of battle, rolled the waters back, caused time to stand still, brought famine and brought rain, turned beggars into preachers, and caused many who were sick to be healed. Prayer has locked the jaws of lions, brought fire from heaven to consume a sacrifice, and caused the fire of God to fall on humble hearts time and time again.

This prayer of which I speak is not a vain repetition of words composed or read by some careless individual, but the crying out to God of a humble heart, a soul reaching out seeking, asking, pleading for higher plains, for blessings for others or self. A "heaven-moving prayer" must burst from the soul, such as the prayer the blind man prayed in Mark 10:47. His prayer was short, but it brought a quick answer.

Oh! If only the church were to come to her knees today and really pray, what a difference it would make. Churches would fill, altars would fill, and praises would go up to God. What a power we have if we would only use it.

3. *The Power of Purity and Separation.* "Be ye clean that bear the vessel of the Lord" (Isa. 52:11) is meaningful for us today. David said "if I regard iniquity in my heart, the Lord will not hear me." There is no power in a sinful life. We are living in a day of conformity and appeasement. This has been the downfall of many. John the Baptist took the Nazarite vow. This vow was from the kernel to the husks (Num. 6:3). Daniel retained this vow of separation by refusing to drink with the people of Babylon. In Luke 1:15 we are told John the Baptist abstained from wine and worldliness. Let us join together in fervent prayer for a revival of purity and power.

4. *The Power of Love.* Love caused God to send His Son. Love caused Christ to give His life that we might have life and have it more abundantly. Love covers a multitude of faults. Love has a drawing power greater than any other. Love has been known to have drawn a man from one side of the world to the other. God's love will expel fear, bring us together in unity, cure old church sores and many other ills of our day. We need the mastery of this love today.

5. *The Power of Pentecost.* "But ye shall receive power after that the Holy Ghost is come upon you and ye shall be witnesses unto me" (Acts 1:8). The gift which Christ prayed the Father to send upon us has come. First upon the one hundred and twenty in the upper room (Acts 2), later upon others at Cornelius's house, at Ephesus and other places down through the ages. But God does not fill unclean temples with His Spirit. The blood of cleansing touched the thumb, ear and toe of the high priest before he ministered. According to the statement of James in Acts 15:9, the Apostles were refined and purified before being filled with the Spirit at Pentecost. Every one needs this power to witness, power to live a victorious life before others, power to study and interpret God's Word, that we might be vessels for God to use. We need all God's gifts for the upbuilding of His kingdom.

6. *The Power of the Resurrection.* We mention this last, but it is not least. Many people seldom think of there being a resurrection

power. Yet in order for a body to be brought forth from the grave, from the tomb, from the sea, from the crevices of the earth and mountains, and in order for the living redeemed to be changed in a moment, there must be great resurrection power. This is the moment all we as saints of God look forward to. This is that blessed hope for which we live — Christ the first-fruits and afterwards they that are Christ's at His coming. But, says Paul, "every one in his own order," or rank (1 Cor. 15:23). "Blessed and holy is he that hath part in the first resurrection: on such the second death hath no power" (Rev. 20:6).

Thank God for this power which some day will snatch us away forever to be with God in that land of wonder and beauty. While we are thinking of our home over there, let us use all these powers for the glory of God and His kingdom.

ONE FEARLESS PREACHER

John the Baptist who came on the scene at the end of a dying dispensation, and the Apostle Peter who appears at the beginning of the new dispensation, both illustrate and epitomize the doctrine of spiritual fullness. The prophecies which foretell the outpouring of the Spirit in the Old Testament both focus and operate in the ministry of these two men. Everything claimed elsewhere in these writings are found to be workable in them. They show (or prove) their faith by their works (James 2:18).

Consider John the Baptist. Scriptures concerning him are John 1:1-39; Luke 3:1-22; Matt. 3:1-17; John 3:22, 23; Matt. 11:2-19.

These scriptures show he was an evangelist, preacher and prophet. He was the most picturesque person of his time. He was a country preacher of strange birth, a mountain giant raised in the hills and fed on locust and wild honey. He was poorly clad, with long hair, bare arms and legs. His voice thundered God's dynamic denunciation of hypocrisy, but his voice was soft as a love-call in urging sinners to repent. He was God-sent and Spirit-filled. His pulpit was the mountain sides of Judea, his auditorium was the valleys and vaulted skies, his audiences made up of all sorts of people, publicans, sinners, Pharisees, scribes, Sadducees, soldiers—people from city, plain and mountains. Kings and governors came to listen and went away to fear. He was great in tenderness, lion-like in boldness, simple, pungent, convincing, powerful like a storm out of the mountains. He was no crooner, prima-donna, or apologist. He was God's prophet of a new day and coming kingdom.

His was the voice of a strange and new message: sin, repentance, faith, confession, God's Messiah-Lamb ready for sacrifice, baptism, a new doctrine of redemption by death with resurrection hope and Holy Ghost power. He brought in a new day for dying men.

His ministry was short, estimated by our Biblical chronologists as from six to twenty-four months, but how meaningful to the world's destiny! He overturned the traditions of centuries. He brought multitudes to the light and introduced the Light of the ages to men everywhere. One of the saddest tragedies in all spiritual history is his death at the hands of a drunken king to satisfy an outraged woman.

His commission is outlined for us in Luke 1:15-17, 67-80. He was a God-called, Spirit-filled soul-winner: (1) to make ready a people to receive their Redeemer; (2) to turn the hearts of the children to their fathers, and the fathers to the children; and (3) to introduce the world's Saviour.

His message and manner seem to have been clear in thought and powerful in words. His message was crashing and cutting. His humility was touching. He was willing to decrease that Christ might increase. In his humility he was unworthy to unlatch Christ's shoes, but in his personality and ministry powerful enough to empty the cities to hear him.

He only feared God's disapproval. He told kings their sins and faced soldiers and high dignitaries with their sins. His messages were burning and shining. They were hot with holy fires.

His preaching was vibrant with vital doctrines wonderfully brought out in the Gospels following him. He painted sin black and hell-deserving. He demanded repentance, soul moving and heart cleansing, bringing fruit in life and conduct, and baptism that proclaimed repentance from sin and a new step into a life of service for God. He preached the atonement. He called Christ God's Lamb and pictured the atonement in the new ordinance of baptism which he introduced by God's authority. He preached the baptism of the Holy Ghost and enduement of power for world conquering service.

What made him great?

1. God's call and the Spirit's leadership.
2. A life of separation from sin, supplication and communion with God.
3. An unselfish humility and fearless courage.
4. A mighty grip upon the vital truths of God.
5. His compassion for the lost that caused him to face peril and endure any sacrifice in order to win them to God.
6. The great way the Spirit filled and used him. He yielded to God's leadership in childhood and remained in his Father's will until his head was carried to a wicked queen on a charger.

While his span of life was brief, yet marvelous conclusions are gathered from it. Life in its eternal meaning does not consist in meat and drink, clothes nor earthly honor, nor even in space of years. Place his life beside that of Methuselah who lived nearly one thousand years. But during the wide expanse of time nothing is recorded of his accomplishments and he lived a thin life. We conclude life consists in doing God's will in His time and place! John's life lived in the hills of Judea, in a remote age, has cast golden glory and radiant hope to all succeeding generations. God's Word says this simple country preacher was the greatest born of woman (Matt. 11:11). He introduced the Saviour to a ruined world and pointed men to the Lamb of God that takes away sin (John 1:29).

We can preach the same Gospel in the power of the same Spirit, and walk the way of favor and glory.

PART I

HELPS FOR SPECIAL OCCASIONS

FUNERAL REMINDERS

The ability to conduct a smooth service with a message full of sympathy and heart power is a tremendous asset to a minister. Any average minister can do this. The following suggestions have been used by the writer in as many as five funerals in one day. With a sincere prayer to be helpful, we pass to you the following suggestions.

When a death occurs in the *flock,* or among people with no church connection, it is in the minister's own interest as that of the family in sorrow, that he call at once. Very seldom will his advice be asked, but the wishes of the bereaved will be given. The minimum expected of him will be a prayer and an address. His *manner* should be *sympathetic, subdued* and *tender.*

Most funeral sermons are too long. The Shepherd can give the "comfort of the scriptures" (Rom. 15:4) without being lengthy. Fashions in funerals change. We are now in a decade when the trend is away from obituaries. Many well-managed funerals omit them. Now hymns are often read by the minister instead of sung. But we recommend a brief obituary, giving a sketch only of the life of the deceased, and truthfully relating incidents and features of interest to the audience.

There is no such thing as a "non-personal" funeral. We call attention to two sermons in the following group. I. Funeral of a Child, and, 2. The Funeral of the Unsaved. These are the most difficult to conduct. We start them with a prayer, not a full length one, but a substantial invocation. The purpose of this is quickly to bring the atmosphere which belongs to the occasion and set the tone of the service. Conditions, such as weather and comfort, require rituals at the graveside to be brief.

THE FUNERAL OF A CHILD

"And they brought young children to him, that he should touch them; and his disciples rebuked them that brought them. But when Jesus saw it, he was much displeased, and said unto them, Suffer the little children to come unto me, and forbid them not; for of such is the kingdom of God. And he took them up in his arms . . . and blessed them" (Mark 10:13, 14, 16).

Prayer:

Our Heavenly Father, God of all comfort, look with compassion upon the sorrowing hearts gathered here, especially upon these parents whose joy has been turned to sorrow. They have drunk of the cup of bitterness; wilt Thou now give them the cup of consolation? Let not their faith die, nor their light go out in darkness. Give them the spirit of Him who learned obedience by the things which He suffered, so that like Him, they too may say in meekness and submission, "Not my will but thine be done." Comfort them with the assurance their loved one is at peace and rest and will be remembered in the day when Thou dost return to make up Thy jewels. In this hour of trial draw Thy servants near and help them to trust and believe that deeper than the pain of separation are the everlasting arms of strength and mercy. Grant us an answer to our prayer in the Name of Jesus who is the Mediator between God and man. Amen.

Message:

Sacred memories cluster around the birth and death of a child. At the birth of a child joys unknown to others are stirred in the hearts of the parents. A new world of affection is opened within them. At his death, their hearts feel a shock and loss such as they have never before known. Our prayer today is that the Holy Scriptures may speak words of comfort to them. My object is to lead these afflicted parents to feel that it is well with them and their departed child.

"The Lord hath need of it" (Mark 11:3). A hint of why it was called out of this world may be seen in what is said in Revelation 14:3, "And they sung . . . a new song . . . and no man could learn that song. . . ." Why could no one else but they themselves sing this song? Because it is the song of innocence, swelling out from heavenly voices and reverberating through the world. Yes, the Bible says they were redeemed from among men. That means they once belonged to the earth. They enjoyed the benefits of the Atonement and the victory of redemption. They are pure and undefiled, strangers to the kind of sins we have committed. In their mouth is no guile; they stand before the throne of God without spot, blemish, wrinkle or any such thing. God calls whom He wills to join this heavenly chorus.

Unutterable glory in the death of children. Christ says in Matthew 21:16, "Out of the mouths of babes and sucklings thou hast perfected praise." Heaven is a world of music and singing. Harps are being played (Rev. 14:2). David the sweet singer of Israel may be leading a choir in heaven a million strong. Who knows but what children are in that temple choir furnishing charm and beauty to that world of light?

David said when his child was taken in death, "I shall go to him, but he shall not return to me" (2 Sam. 12:23). He believed they would be together. In the faith of a sure reunion in that happy world, we give up our dead.

At the grave:

The following scriptures are suitable reading at the graveside. Ps. 46; 121; John 11:23-26; 2 Cor. 4:8-18; 5:1-8; Rev. 21:1-6.

Prayer:

O Lord our God, we come to Thee in this hour in the Name of Jesus, Thine only begotten Son. Our spirits turn to Thee in humble trust and submission. Amid the decay of visible things, draw nigh unto our fainting souls. As these changes in life leave us poor and sad, hold not Thy peace at our tears, but come with the balm of Thy presence and heal our broken hearts. Comfort Thy sorrowing children. Grant them grace to return home in the faith of a victorious resurrection and a glorious reunion with their departed loved one. Enable them to serve their day and generation, and may they so live as to be united with those gone before in that eternal city of light, through Jesus Christ our blessed Lord. Amen.

Committal:

"I heard a voice from heaven saying, Write, Blessed are the dead which die in the Lord, from henceforth, yea, saith the Spirit, that they may rest from their labors and their works do follow them."

In the faith of our Lord Jesus Christ, who took little children in His arms and blessed them, we commit to the tomb the body of this child, in the assurance that his immortal spirit is at home with the Heavenly Father.

"They shall be mine saith the Lord of Hosts, in that day when I make up my jewels." We believe that in death as in life they are in Thy Holy keeping and ever shall be until that eternal morning when Christ returns and the righteous dead and living shall be changed in a moment and raised to forever be with the Lord.

Benediction.

"The Lord bless thee and keep thee: the Lord make His face to shine upon thee, and be gracious unto thee, the Lord lift up His countenance upon thee and give thee peace." Amen.

THE FUNERAL OF THE UNSAVED

"The last enemy that shall be destroyed is death" (1 Cor. 15:26).

Prayer:

Heavenly Father, we know there is help for all in Thy Name. We know there is shelter from the storm and heat of life. Remember the hearts who are shocked by death and smitten by its power. Hear our prayers for those who are mourning today. Touch their wounds with Thy healing balm. May the comforting scriptures speak in the homes of silence and fill those empty chairs. Make Thy people to know that the eternal God is our refuge and that underneath are the everlasting arms, for we ask in Jesus' Name, Amen.

Message:

Death is often disguised by poetic description and figures of speech. But after death is woven in a web of words by wizards of language, the fact remains that death is a terrible enemy. It has been preying on humanity since the days of Adam and Eve. We are told in our text of a day when it shall be destroyed. But that day has not yet arrived. Today death is on the loose! Money cannot bribe it, strength cannot defy it, or power defeat it. It is an enemy blind to our tears, deaf to our prayers, unmindful of our grief. It has invaded homes and carried our loved ones away to a gloomy prison house of decay. The more we see of death's dreadful dealings with the race, the more we dread its approach and shun its presence. It has no mercy on the youth, the hoary head of age, nor the shoulders bent with the burden of years. It has filled the world with lamentations and left it black with mourning. Its pathway is wet with tears and dotted with graves. When it comes, it deals out to us the cup of bitterness and woe.

Mothers have knelt before the death angel and pleaded for their children; sisters have bowed at his iron throne and begged in vain for their brothers; whole churches and nations have failed to move him to one deed of compassion.

Other conquerors have lived a while and died. Caesar, Alexander and Napoleon are slumbering in their graves. For a short time their banners waved over defeated armies and prostrated empires, but the time of their triumph was short. The solemn funeral dirges sounded over their graves but, they heard it not. Their dust has mingled with the ashes of beggars and slaves. But death is not yet destroyed. Its monuments dot the road of life for a distance of six thousand years. It marked our first parents as victims. It struck down the Patriarchs, prophets and kings. Death sent their ashes to the sepulcher. At midnight and mid-noon it has spread its black pinions over hovels and mansions alike. The millionaire and the hobo have come down to common graves.

Death does not come in the same form to all. The Patriarch Job said, "Now my days are swifter than a post; they flee away, they see no good" (Job 9:25-28). He did not compare his days to a slow caravan which traveled only two or three miles an hour, but to a messenger riding in full gallop carrying a proclamation from the king. By this he shows how rapidly man's days were spent. Death comes in a violent form to some, while to others it comes in a lingering, wasting disease.

Christ came to abolish death and to give life and immortality through the Gospel (2 Tim. 1:10). He came to seal forever the mouth of the sepulcher and to end the dominion of the grave. John 5:28, 29 says, "Marvel not at this, the hour is coming when all that are in the graves shall hear the voice of the Son of man and come forth." Christ proved His victory over the grave by raising the ruler's daughter, the widow's son, and also Lazarus from the dead. His own resurrection is a proof and pledge of our own that is coming. The last enemy that shall be destroyed is death.

Let me announce to you as mildly as I can that you are about to exchange worlds. Only faith in God and trust in Jesus, the Conqueror, can remove the terror and sorrow of the tomb for you. Death can become a friend to help you pass through the gates to eternal light and happiness. You are coming to the end. How many opportunities to be saved have you had? One day you will have the last one! Lot's wife did! She is a monument to those who waited too long. Some day you will speak your last word and take your last look at the blue sky and the green earth. You will glance around the room at the faces you love. The last breath will be drawn. Your heart will flutter a little and life will stop. You will be dead! Will you be ready? You are the only one who decides which place, heaven or hell, shall be your eternal home. May you decide rightly . . . and now!

At the grave:

"The Lord knoweth our frame; He remembereth that we are dust. As for man, his days are as grass: as a flower of the field, so he flourisheth. For the wind passeth over it, and it is gone; and the place thereof shall know it no more."

"Man cometh forth as a flower; and is cut down; he fleeth also as a shadow, and continueth not."

Since the earthly pilgrimage of ____________ (*give name of the deceased*) hath ended in the silent city of the dead, and since we brought nothing into this world and it is certain we can carry nothing out, it becomes our sad duty to commit (his, or her) remains to the tomb, ashes to ashes, and dust to dust, and the spirit we commit to God who gave it, in the assurance that He who is the Judge of all the earth shall do right.

Benediction:

Upon the family and friends that remain we say, "The Lord bless you and keep you; the Lord make His face to shine upon you, and be gracious unto you: the Lord lift up His countenance upon you and give you peace." Amen.

THE FUNERAL OF A CHRISTIAN

"For to me to live is Christ, and to die is gain. For I am in a strait betwixt two, having a desire to depart and be with Christ; which is far better" (Phil. 1:21-23).

Prayer:

Heavenly Father, one by one Thou dost gather the scattered families out of the earthly life into the heavenly glory, out of the strife and turmoil of time into the peace of eternity. We thank Thee for the labors and joys of these mortal years. We thank Thee for the inheritance of Thy children, and for the eye of faith Thou hast opened for us, so we like Moses can have "respect unto the recompense of reward." We thank Thee for the light and lives of those who have shone in the several generations of the world. We here today remember Thy holy prophets and apostles and a "great multitude which no man can number," who have departed this life with the seal of faith upon them. We ask for strength and stedfastness to continue in victorious faith 'til we hear Thy call to come up higher. We ask this through Jesus Christ our Lord. Amen.

Message:

All we have to do to see the bright side of death is to look again at the words of Jesus in John 11:25, 26, "I am the resurrection and the life; he that believeth in me, though he were dead, yet shall he live. And whosoever liveth and believeth in me shall never die." These words are both specific and revealing. They come from the Master of eternity.

1. *Jesus taught that believers would never die.* Death (separation of soul from the body) is a transition. It is the passing from an old body, which is no longer able to serve us, into a new, spiritual body. Paul says in 1 Cor. 15:44, "There is a natural body, and there is a spiritual body." Our spiritual and intelligent parts are imperishable. The will, affections, and conscience—those things which make up the human personality—continue on. The soul is more real than the house it lives in. Death does not, and cannot, destroy the inhabitant of the body. Paul tells us in 1 Cor. 15:26 that death itself shall be destroyed. Death, or what we call death, only takes down the house in which the believer lives. The faithful believer never dies (John 11:26). Man was created immortal and he shall rise from the grave and live forever. "This mortal shall put on immortality."

2. Death is a "change" (Job 14:14). It is the gateway of life and the vestibule of heaven. With the Christian it is moving from the gloom of life to eternal daylight. It is going from what is good of earth to the best in the Father's house. Paul says in Rom. 8:23, "We groan within ourselves waiting for the adoption, to wit, the redemption of the body." Death is the Christian's deliverance from bondage and limitations – such as a deformed, sick and decaying body, which mars life's pleasures and happiness – into the glorious liberty of the children of God. It is going from small to larger opportunities. It is like one who moves from the poorhouse to the king's palace, from eating hard-tack to everlasting banquetings. It is leaving a few friends here and going to dwell with that "innumerable company of angels," and where the spirits of just men reach perfection (Heb. 12:22, 23, Berkeley Version). Death is the Christian's last conflict before receiving his crown.

3. We are going to have new homes. Jesus said in John 14:2, "I go to prepare a place for you." Any occupied space is a "place." Heaven is a real place. Paul says "to be absent from the body is to be present with the Lord." Consequently, death is a home-going for the believer. When we close our eyes here and open them in that better world, we shall find that we are not among strangers but among those we have loved and lost for a while.

In ancient times it is said of Jacob that "he was gathered to his people" (Gen. 49:33). A similar statement was made concerning

David and his young son who died, "I shall go to him, but he shall not return to me" (2 Sam. 12:23).

What will heaven be like? It will not be like this earth which has been cursed with sin and blighted by a multitude of evils. No heavy burdens will weigh on tired shoulders in that world of comfort and beauty. Cheeks will never turn pale, and eyes will never set in glassy stare. There will be no crepe, no undertakers and hearses. There will be no heartbreaking moments when caskets are lowered and clods go falling down, for, "God shall wipe away all tears from their eyes; and there will be no more death, neither sorrow nor crying: neither shall there be any more pain" (Rev. 21:4).

Paul mentions heaven as a place of light. In 1 Tim. 6:16 he speaks of the King of Kings and Lord of Lords as "dwelling in the light which no man can approach unto, whom no man hath seen nor can see." That refers to seeing with the human eye. But in heaven we shall see face to face (1 Cor. 13:14). Paul at one time had the privilege of looking into Paradise, where he saw wonderful things. He was forbidden to tell these things (lest people would want to leave this world before their time) but we do know he did say, "having a desire to depart and be with Christ; which is far better" (Phil. 1:23). That is just another way of saying, "If I had my way about it, I'd rather leave right now."

Heaven is a busy place. A heaven where we had nothing to do but sit beside the crystal seas and gaze forever on the eternal beauty and dazzling glory of the world about us might be suitable for mystics and dreamers, but not for us who love activity. There we will meet and know people who have lived in the different generations of time. Conversations with men like Joseph, Daniel and Job, will be entrancing; crowns will be awarded to the faithful; but the grandest thing of all will be that Jesus who loved and redeemed us from every tribe, kindred and tongue will be there.

It seems to me I shall never get through looking at Him. I will want to thank Him for bringing me there. I will thank Him for letting me preach His Word. I will tell Him I am sorry I did not do it better.

When mothers and fathers, sons and daughters all go out and sit down in some bright, restful spot together, what a time of reunion that will be. It is a blessed thing to know that in the next life God offers us what we long for here — a body not subject to age, disease, pain, death, plus a soul capable of enjoyment in coming ages. So we come to the end of the way and are glad to lay aside an old worn-out body which no longer serves us, just as we are glad to dispense with a worn-out garment to receive a new one. Paul tells us in 1 Cor. 15:44, "There is a natural body and there is a spiritual body," and in verse 49 he tells us, "As we have borne the image of the earthy we shall also bear the image of the heavenly."

Heaven is an eternal place. What has become of some of the great cities this earth has known? Where is Nineveh? Where is Carthage? Where is Babylon? Gone! Perished! But heaven is a place, "whose builder and Maker is God," whose foundations shall never crumble away. Paul says, "We have no continuing city, but we seek one to come," and that city, thank God, will continue forever and ever.

At the grave:

Psa. 34:19, "Many are the afflictions of the righteous, but the Lord delivereth him out of them all."

2 Cor. 4:17, "For our light affliction, which is but for a moment, worketh for us a far more exceeding and eternal weight of glory."

Rev. 14:13, "I heard a voice from heaven saying, Write, blessed are the dead which die in the Lord from henceforth; Yea, saith the Spirit, that they may rest from their labors and their works do follow them."

Prayer:

Our Father who art in heaven, Thou hast said, "Blessed are they that mourn, for they shall be comforted. Blessed are they that do hunger and thirst after righteousness, for they shall be filled." We give thanks for the life and example of this Thy servant whom Thou hast called from the "household of faith" to join the blood-washed throngs in the presence of the Lamb. Comfort and uphold those of his (or her) loved ones left behind. May they find in Thee their refuge and faith to face the future with confidence and hope. Through Jesus Christ our Lord, Amen.

Committal:

For as much as God in His wise providence hath taken from this life the soul of our deceased (*brother, sister*) it becomes our sad duty to commit (*his* or *her*) body to the tomb and commend (*his* or *her*) spirit unto Him who gave it. "For we know that if our earthly house of this tabernacle be dissolved, we have a building of God, a house not made with hands, eternal in the heavens."

We give Thee thanks for the victory of Christ over death and the grave and for His words, "because I live ye shall live also."

Keep us, who are still in the body, along with all that are around Thee in heaven, in union with Him who is the Resurrection and the Life, who liveth and reigneth with Thee, world without end, Amen.

Benediction:

THE FUNERAL OF AN AGED PERSON

"The hoary head is a crown of glory, if it be found in the way of righteousness" (Prov. 16:31).

Prayer:

Heavenly Father, we come to Thee because we need Thy help. Make us to realize that in Thy holy care are all Thy children, whether here or there; that the Eternal God is our refuge and that underneath are the everlasting arms. In this hour hear our prayers for those who are mourning for their dead. May Thy healing balm touch their wounds and give them strength to do and bear Thy perfect will. Help them to live bravely for the sake of their departed loved one, whose memory we honor and cherish in this hour. We pray in Jesus' Name, Amen.

Message:

The most delightful glimpses of childhood are found in the Bible. Nothing is more touching than the account of Samuel's little coat made by his mother's own hands and presented to him in the temple; or the lad with loaves and fishes giving his possessions to Christ for use; or Moses, God's gift to Israel and to the world, set afloat in the little basket ark; or the little ones whom Jesus gathered to His breast as He said, "of such is the kingdom of heaven." We are permitted to bend over the cradle of many a new-born babe and share the joy of the parents, for God taught the Jews that children were His gift, and a mark of His favor.

But old age has its place in the sacred record. Our aged friends can rejoice because they are not omitted. We follow Joshua till he is 85 years old, Moses till 120, Jacob till 149, Isaac till 180, Enoch till 365, and Noah till 950. God never forgets His children. Old age, even of the sinful and immoral, is spoken of tenderly, sympathetically. "The beauty of an old man is the grey head."

Not all in this house today have come to life's evening. For many the sun still lingers in the morning sky. Others have reached the high-tide of life and vigor. For some it may be a day of storms. I doubt not that your lives have seen a full measure of sorrow and strife, but as you look back over the past, you can see the brightness of the Father's love, and every sorrow glistens with the rays of His comfort. You have tested the truth of the scripture, "The hoary head is a crown of glory, if it be found in the way of righteousness."

1. There is a beauty and sweetness about life's sunset not observed by many. No hour of the day is more inspiring and becalming than the hour of sunset. The day is done. The fervor of its shining is over, and the sun hangs in the golden west making everything look unspeakably beautiful. The very atmosphere partakes of the glory of the departing day. Weary laborers repose. Children leave their play to gather in the home for the evening prayer and blessing. It is time for rest, prayer and sleep. William the Conqueror introduced into England the ringing of the curfew bells. The curfew meant all fires should be extinguished, and all people should retire for rest. For some here today, curfew will soon sound. The fires of life will be banked, and they will go to sleep. Whether their portion will be rest and glory will depend on whether the "hoary head will be found in the way of righteousness."

2. Joseph Jennings, of sacred memory, when on the verge of that world of wonder and beauty, looking over exclaimed, "Beautiful. What a morning." His weeping wife, not seeing what he saw, said, "Shall I open the shutters to give you a better view?" "Oh!" he said, "I have looked a great way beyond the shutters." He was in the dawn of the next world.

Those who do not look beyond the shutters of old age are being robbed of their birthright. Plan and zest and work belong to this world's busy life. This is not the time and place to wait for time to run out and eternity to begin. Do as Christ said, "Work while it is day, for the night cometh when no man can work." Many of your acquaintances have already been taken, friends and loved ones as well as foes. Behold, the aged one now stands like a giant of the forest out in the open, swept by every wind and bruised by every storm. You may feel all paths have closed save one, the path to the tomb. You may feel the world has nothing for you, and you have nothing for the world. This can only be true of those who do not look "beyond the shutters." Can you conceive of a sadder picture—life all but lived; the world fast receding; earthly ties snapping; barely more than two strands binding to the present, and no certainty of what lies beyond, around, beneath?

Dr. A. J. Gordon met an aged man going to the place of prayer, "Aged friend, how is it that so old a man is so cheerful?" He replied, "Because I belong to the Lord." "Are others happy at your age?" The aged gentleman replied, "Listen to the truth from one who knows, then tell it everywhere, and no man of three score and ten can gainsay it — the devil has no happy old men."

3. But the picture has another side. If many things are gone, many more remain. The aged Christian has passed beyond the most hazardous periods and scenes of life. He is unaffected by some of the most pernicious influences of a bad world. The world has not lost its influences over him simply because his physical powers have weakened, but because he has learned to put right value on things.

The aged Christian has reserved to him the most powerful agency in life — prayer! A noted minister once said, "More things are wrought by prayer than this world dreams of." We should never dwell in our places of worship without thinking of the score or more members whose weight of years denies them the privilege of being there, but who never fail to pray for the pastor and the church. The aged Christian may fully lean on Jesus. Herein is his privilege and joy. How beautiful is old age when cheered by the presence and power of the Almighty! There are no fears and anxieties about the future. He is leaning on the everlasting arms.

The aged Christian can witness for Christ. Life's evening will take its character from the days which have preceded it. In this connection the words of Solomon carry tremendous weight: "Remember now thy Creator in the days of thy youth, while the evil days come not, nor the years draw nigh, when thou shalt say, I have no pleasure in them" (Eccl. 12:1). If we are to come to life's close with the comfort of Christian hope, we must prepare for it while it is yet day.

In the glory of life's evening David sang: "The Lord is my light and my salvation; whom shall I fear? The Lord is the strength of my life, of whom shall I be afraid?" (Psa. 27:1). Is this the song of a man trusting in the dark? No! He had come to know God's love and power, not from others, but in the trials and conflicts of his own life. He had come off a conqueror through God's grace. Dark clouds of danger overhung his youth, but through them he had come to know the silver lining of God's protection. David's trust was founded upon conquest over terrible sin. He was strengthened by comfort after bitter sorrow, and confirmed by succeeding years of spiritual growth and enlargement.

In the closing days of Paul's life he exclaimed: "Who shall separate us from the love of Christ? Shall tribulation, or peril, or persecution, or famine, or nakedness, or distress or sword?" Could Paul have said that in the morning days of his life? No! Could he have said that if his life had been one of luxury and ease? You know he could not! The silver crown may well tell of sacrifice, toil, and burdens bravely borne. Shall white hair be a crown of glory? This is the ripening time of life. It is better further on. Gladly we greet the white messenger and with faith keep on our pilgrimage. To those who may be out of Christ, it is still not too late. Even for such we say, "Now is the accepted time" (2 Cor. 6:2).

At the grave:

Suitable scriptures to be read are: Job 24:22-24; 2 Chron. 32:33; 2 Chron. 35:24, 25.

Prayer:

O God of our Fathers, we thank Thee for the battles fought and the victories won. Thou hast said, "The hoary head is a crown of glory, if it be found in the way of righteousness." In this consecrated burying ground today we give Thee thanks for the holy triumphs of Thy saints in every age and among all peoples. Bless all old people everywhere: some have wandered far in life's pathway and some have forgotten Thee. Turn, we pray Thee, their trembling steps into the ways of righteousness. The young may die, but the old must! Prepare all hearts for this change.

O Lord, we beseech Thee to bless all these relatives and friends in their grief and sorrow. At this time of separation may they come to know Thee better and learn to rely upon Thy unchanging love. May the lessons and examples of Thy servants who have died in the faith be remembered in the years that are to come, for we ask all in Jesus' Name. Amen.

Committal:

"We brought nothing into this world and it is certain we can carry nothing out."

"I heard a voice from heaven saying, Write, Blessed are the dead which die in the Lord, from henceforth, Yea, saith the Spirit, that they may rest from their labors, and their works do follow them."

For as much as the spirit of this departed one hath returned to God who gave it, it becomes our sad duty tenderly to commit the body to the earth, in the faith and certain hope of the resurrection at which time all the dead in Christ shall arise and stand with Christ and hear the welcome summons, "Enter into the joys of the Lord." For His is the kingdom, and the power and the glory, forever, Amen.

Benediction:

A MARRIAGE CEREMONY

Friends, because of the sacredness and great meaning of marriage, I shall take a moment to tell you what the Bible says about it.

The rite of marriage in which you two come now to be united is the oldest religious rite in the world. It was instituted by God while man was in his innocency. Man fell but marriage did not. What it was at the beginning, it is now. Marriage has never fallen. It has been continued by God to soothe the sorrows and comfort the broken estate of man. The Lord said, "It is not good that the man should be alone; I will make an help meet for him." Again He said, "They two shall be one."

The Apostle Paul said "marriage is honorable in all." Jesus Christ honored and sanctioned the wedding in Cana of Galilee with His presence, and it was there that He wrought His first miracle, bringing cheer and joy to the host and his guests. In thus beatifying this earthly union of marriage by His first recorded manifestation of miracle-working power, Christ shows that He saw in it a symbol of the day to come when He, Himself, as the blessed heavenly bridegroom of the church, should lead His own "beloved," the mystical bride chosen and drawn by grace from among men, to that great marriage supper of the Lamb.

In creation Adam, the man, was first formed, then Eve, says the scripture, that the woman might be for the man. Yet, man in being made last of all God's creative works, was set forth as the most excellent of all God's creatures. So Eve, the woman, being made after Adam and out of him has the honor set upon her as being the glory of man.

As the man is the head, she is the crown, a crown to her husband. The man is dust refined, but she is dust doubly refined or one step further from the earth. But in being created from man, or out of him, she was not out of his head to dominate him or to be over him, nor out of his feet to be under him or to be trampled upon by him, but out of his side to be equal with him, from under his arm to be protected by him, and near his heart to be loved by him.

Into this holy estate you two come now to be united.

Invocation here (but not full length prayer):

To the Groom:

Will you have this woman to be your wedded wife, to live together after God's ordinance, in the holy state of matrimony? Will you love her, honor and keep her in sickness and in health, and, forsaking all others, keep yourself only to her so long as you live, so help you God? (*Groom answers*) I will.

(*Then shall the minister say*) Who gives this woman to be married to this man?

(*The bride's escort shall say*) I do (*Here the escort withdraws to be seated with the family.*)

(*Minister says to groom*) You may now take the bride's hand.

(*The groom repeats after the minister as follows*) I take thee to be my wedded wife, to have and to hold from this day forward, for better, for worse, for richer or poorer, in sickness and in health, to love and to cherish, till death do us part.

(*The bride repeats after the minister as follows*) I take thee to be my wedded husband, to have and to hold from this day forward, for better, for worse, for richer or poorer, in sickness and in health, to love and to cherish, till death do us part.

Ring Ceremony:

When God made a covenant with Noah, He set a rainbow in the cloud and said, "I will look upon it that I may remember it was an everlasting covenant." So from this we learn it is well for us, when entering solemn agreements, to set aside some token as a reminder. You have, therefore, chosen these rings as the token of your marriage covenant. They are made of gold and become a type of that which is the least easily tarnished and the most enduring, and fitly represent the ties that bind husband and wife together. These rings are an endless circle, until broken by some outside force, and are a symbol of the unbroken marriage union which God has ordained and shall continue until broken only by death.

(*Minister to the groom*) Take this ring and place it upon the fourth finger of her left hand. Let this ring be the seal of your mutual love and fidelity, and a memorial of this sacred service. You will repeat the following after me: "With this ring I thee wed, and with all my worldly goods I thee endow, in the Name of the Father, and the Son and the Holy Ghost." (*Minister to the bride*) Place this ring on the fourth finger of his left hand and repeat the following: "With this ring I thee wed, and with all my love and honor I thee endow, in the Name of the Father, and the Son, and the Holy Ghost." (*Where bride does not give a ring, she says,* "I receive this ring and with all my love and honor I thee endow, in the Name of the Father, and of the Son, and of the Holy Ghost".) Now let me speak to your hearts. I charge you both as you hope for happiness in your married life to be true to the vows you have made each to the other. With your marriage from this day you begin life anew with larger responsibilities.

(*Minister to the groom*) Guard well this your bride who now commits herself into your keeping, and strive to live that no words or deeds of yours shall ever cloud her brow with grief or dim her eyes with tears.

(*Minister to the bride*) It will be your part to strive to retain by your virtues the heart you have won by your graces.

And to you both, I would say, let not your voices lose the tender tones of affection, nor your eyes forget the tender ray with which they shone in courtship's day. And greatest of all, let God be enthroned in your home and in your hearts above all else and at all times.

Prayer (standing or on kneeling board):

And now having heard you make these pledges of your affection and take these vows of fidelity, I do by authority vested in me by the laws of the State of ____________________ and the Church of ____________________, pronounce you husband and wife, no longer twain, but now one, in the Name of the Father and of the Son and of the Holy Ghost. Amen.

"That which God hath joined together, let not man put asunder."

Groom salutes the bride with a "holy kiss."

Benediction (Numbers 6:24-26).

Congratulations:

A GOLDEN WEDDING ANNIVERSARY CEREMONY

While this is largely a social affair, ministers are often invited to participate. If on this occasion the wedding vows and re-consecration of the marriage is desired, the ceremony can be somewhat as follows:

We have met together in the sight of God and in the presence of this company of witnesses to aid this man and wife in renewing their marriage vows which they took fifty years ago. The long and happy married life with faith, love, and devotion to each other for half a century, with which they have been blessed, has also blessed us who know them best.

After a successful and happy married life for fifty years, they stand here to bear witness that the marriage law instituted by God is honorable and holy; that married life in the home is happy, sacred, and beautiful; and that it should not be entered into unadvisedly or lightly, but reverently, discreetly, advisedly, soberly, and in the fear of God. They come now again to renew that covenant taken fifty years ago. In the sight of God and in the presence of this company they give each other their heart and hand.

(To the man) Mr. _______________, fifty years ago you took this woman, whose hand you now hold, to be your lawful wedded wife, to live with her in the holy estate of matrimony. You promised to love, comfort, and serve her, to stand by her in sickness and health, forsaking all others, and that you would cling to her and to her alone as long as you both should live. For fifty years you have been faithful to this pledge. Will you, in the presence of your children and grandchildren, and in the presence of this company gathered here, renew these vows and continue your devotion to her as long as you both shall live, so help you God?

Answer: I will.

(To the woman) Mrs. _______________, fifty years ago you took this man, whose hand you now hold, to be your lawful wedded husband, to live with him in the holy estate of matrimony. You promised to love, comfort, and serve him, to stand by him in sickness and health, forsaking all others, and that you would cleave to him and to him alone as long as you both should live. For fifty years you have been faithful to this pledge. Will you, therefore, now in the presence of your children, in the presence of your grandchildren, and in the presence of this company gathered here renew these vows and continue your devotion to him as long as you both shall live?

Answer: I will.

Note: If the ring is to be used, the man presents the ring as in the original ceremony and the original ring should be used. It is only rarely this can be done.

A CORNERSTONE LAYING CEREMONY

"Are built upon the foundation of the apostles and prophets, Jesus Christ himself being the chief cornerstone" (Eph. 2:20).

Palestine is a land of stone. All kinds of stone are there, everything from soft limestone to flint. Both are there in abundance. Stone is put to every conceivable use by the people. A speaker is well understood when he mentions stone. In building, a cornerstone knits together the two walls at the corner.

I. *Christ is the headstone of the corner in the Bible* (Matt. 21:42). He is the center and theme of the Bible. Old Testament types and ceremonies point to Christ. To Him gave the prophets witness. Jesus in His person and work, in His mission and offices, in His first and second advent, is the heart and life of the Bible.

As in Italy all roads lead to Rome, it is in the Bible that all paths lead to Christ. All lines converge toward Him and in Him alone are all its prophecies fulfilled.

He who reads intelligently may see Christ upon every page, and see Him walk the highways of the scripture as He once walked the hills of Judea. He is clearly seen in the Gospels and in the Epistles. His inmost soul is bared, and in the book of Revelation His footsteps may be heard coming on the clouds with power and great glory. If the Old is the promise of the New, the New is the promise of the ultimate triumph of Christ Jesus when He shall be declared King of Kings and Lord of Lords. If the Bible is not interesting or understood by men, it is because they do not know Christ or see Him in its pages. Blot out Christ and you blot out the Book. Lose your Bible and you lose Christ.

II. *Jesus is the cornerstone of the church.* For it He died (Eph. 5:25). By Him it was founded. It is the pillar and ground of the truth. Christianity is distinctively a religion of a person. That person is Christ. Take away Buddha from Buddhism and his religion still stands. What is true of Buddha is true of all other religions. But not so with Christ. Take away Christ and Christianity will die. Take away Christ and the church will crumble to ruins.

Jesus is the glory of the church. He is the theme of her sermons, and the object of her worship. To Him we offer prayer. To Him we sing songs of praise. He is the pattern of our lives and the inspiration of our ideals.

The mission of the church is to lift up Christ and draw all men to Him. The church is God's monument to His Son Jesus. Lincoln's monument reminds us of Lincoln. As the Washington Monument reminds us of the Father of Our Country, so the church at large and every little congregation calls to mind the noble life and vicarious death of Jesus Christ. Every little chapel and every gorgeous cathedral tells of Jesus.

Erected on the eastern hillsides, western prairies, and upon the boulevards of every city are places for preaching His gospel. For this purpose we lay the cornerstone of this building today; whose walls are yet to be reared and which will be dedicated to His service. Take away Christ and her glory is departed. He shall be the glory of the temple above, of which the church on earth is but a type. Without Him heaven would be hell and with Him hell would be heaven.

III. *Jesus is the headstone of the corner in civilization.* The old civilizations existed for kings and princes, for the rich and the great, but the civilization of Jesus is for the peasant as well as the king; for the subject as well as the prince; for the illiterate as well as for the learned; for the slave as well as the master.

Compare the war customs of ancient times with those of the present and you will discover that Christianity has robbed it of many of its horrors. You have read of hostile armies which gathered about the city of Troy and the war that followed. Hector came out to meet the foe and fell dead in battle. In accordance with the customs of ancient warfare Achilles attached the dead body of his fallen foe to the axle of his chariot and dragged it three times around the wall of Troy and then threw the mutilated form at the feet of Hector's widow.

That civilization has been replaced by a better one. In the nineteenth century a cruel war ended at Appomattox Courthouse. The victorious army stood face to face with Lee. Hear the interview! "How many men have you?" When the number is told, he said, "Have they any rations?" A negative answer was given. A supply of rations was ordered. "Have you any horses?" "Let them keep them, they will need them on the farm to till the soil and support their families." A supply of seed corn was ordered that they might make a crop the coming year.

The influence of Christ has brought this change in civilization. The great inventions of our age, the hospitals and almshouses and educational institutions and the great reforms of our age are also monuments of His memory and are marks of the progress of the Christ spirit in the world in which we live.

Christ never wrote a book, but He has been the theme of more books than any person that has ever lived. He never composed a song, but He has been the hero of more songs than any other person. In the world of art He is without an equal.

Without Christ we would never have had Handel's "Messiah" nor many of the great masterpieces of music.

Milton, Shakespeare, Tennyson, and Longfellow kindled their

flames at the fire of Christianity. Blot out Christ and you destroy the great oratorios, the masterpieces of art and the world's best literature.

IV. *Jesus is the headstone of the corner in the believer's affections.* Not a few can say He is the chief among ten thousand and the one altogether lovely. Upon love He founded His empire and thousands have died for Him.

The devotion of saints upon earth is like that of the martyrs. No sacrifice is too great for His followers, no burden too heavy and no journey too long. Houses and lands, parents and friends have been given up for His sake. No other name sounds to them as sweet as Jesus. For Him they suffered the scorn and contempt of men. For His name's sake in home and country they carried the gospel to the ends of the earth. For His sake into the darkest and worst places of the earth they go—to icy Greenland, to darkest Africa, to the leper quarters of China, and the "dead man's land" of South America. Were it necessary, they would go back to the "rack and thumb screw" and to the stake, that they might testify of Him.

V. *Jesus is the headstone of the corner in the world at large.* In His march through the ages, Jesus has swept before Him slavery, oppression and corruption of every kind. All other evils shall yet disappear. From the beginning of Genesis until the end of the Revelation we hear the promise and shout the victory. Soon that prophecy shall be fulfilled: "all kings before Him down shall fall; all nations shall His law obey." At the name above every name, "every knee should bow, of things in heaven, and things in earth, and things under the earth; and that every tongue should confess that Jesus Christ is Lord, to the glory of God the Father" (Phil. 2:10, 11).

A CHURCH BUILDING DEDICATION SERMON

Lesson: 2 Chron. 6
Sermon:

There have been many kinds of buildings used as churches since they started. But remember the early or first century Christians did not build churches for the first fifty or sixty years. The Romans who controlled the countries where they lived would not permit it. The Romans outlawed the Christian religion. Christians literally went underground. Church services were held in homes made of mud, stone and brick. Later the humble buildings were replaced with permanent structures, some of which were magnificent cathedrals which have lasted more than one thousand years. Today in Bible Lands where I have traveled you can see foundations of buildings much older; some doubtless were once used as churches.

History relates that when Virginia was first settled they stretched an awning between two trees and held public worship. In Boonesboro, Kentucky, in 1775, Col. Richard Henderson recorded in his diary, "There is a tree under which one hundred or more may be seated. Sunday we are going to have worship services, and that for a bunch of scoundrels who neither believe in God nor the devil, if we are to judge by what they do and say." After people were settled permanently, log-cabin churches were quickly erected, and these in turn gave way to the beautiful edifices, many of which remain to this day.

Today, we have come to dedicate this building. (*Here give information on how the work got its start in this locality.*) We are all happy to have reached the completion of this building, which will shortly be dedicated to God. Yet the church is not the building — but the people. A certain kind of people make the church. The words of the text tell us, "we are living stones, built into a spiritual house." In 1 Corinthians 3:16, Paul tells us, "Know ye not that ye are the temple of the living God, and that the Spirit of God dwelleth in you?" Let us look at this church of living stones.

1. *The Foundation.* It is tremendously important that a building be erected on a firm foundation lest it sag and cracks appear in the walls, or it even topples over. They tell us engineers will not start building a skyscraper until they have digged down to solid rock, even if it is hundreds of feet in depth. These buildings must take the blasts of storms, quakes and the vibrations of earth. So it is with the Christian life. When the Lord Jesus Christ calls us to be His disciples, and we answer that call, He expects us to "endure to the end." Our house of "experience" must be built on the "rock" (Matt. 7:25).

2. *A Firm Foundation is important* in a building which only lasts for a limited number of years. We here today are building for eternity, not with the cold stones of earth, but with "living stones" that will live forever. Therefore, for us, Christ is both the foundation and the cornerstone of our lives. He had a perfect life, divine wisdom and infinite power, so we can safely build on Him. Let's take a glance at the mistakes of others. They teach us something. Solomon built his kingdom largely on wisdom and riches, but his kingdom fell to pieces. Alexander the Great conquered the whole

world while still young, but wept because there were no more worlds to conquer, and drank himself to death at the age of thirty-three. Mohammed laid the foundation of his empire with fire and sword. These proved futile.

3. *The Blue Print Given in the Bible.* God has put down on paper the directions for making a structure of strength and beauty. We shall be wise to follow these directions. The Lord told Moses to "do all things according to the pattern shown him in the mount." If we follow the plumbline of God's Word for our lives and our churches we will not need human props and leaning posts.

4. *Building Material.* Black jacks and dogwood will not make ax handles. We need good material regardless of the size and shape of the building. It is said Bedford stone can withstand pressure of from twelve to seventeen thousand pounds per square foot. Sandstone is softer when quarried, but becomes stronger with age. There are going to come testing times in life, when tremendous pressure is going to be put on us to do evil. Many pitched battles with the devil must be fought, and in that day of war and struggle we will be glad these living stones of ours are made of good material and have the power of great resistance.

It is possible, however, that there can be bad stone. Picture a beautiful church which has, here and there, stones which are crumbling and leaving holes in the walls, such as is often noted in old historic buildings. It is tragic where bad spots can be seen in the lives of Christians, and bad members among those in the church.

Mortar is important because it holds the stones together. Back in ancient times God said in Ezekiel 13:9-11, that His hand is upon the prophets because one built up a wall, and ten others daubed it with untempered mortar and as a result, it shall fall.

Cement is an important element in holding stones together. Our cement is faith, fellowship, common service and loyalty to Christ our living Head. These things will hold Christians together in spite of hardships, persecutions, and even death. In the days when becoming a Christian meant losing a job, breaking up families and friends, losing property and life itself, there was a bond of fellowship which is absolutely unknown today.

5. *The Purpose of the Building.* This building has not been erected merely as an ornament, although it is a credit to the town. It has been placed here to use, and it is of little value unless it is used! In the East today can be found church buildings with a staff well paid, but with only a handful of worshippers.

A situation such as that is almost a mockery. Banks are not open three hours on Saturday, and an hour one evening during the week. You would say, "The business world could not carry on like that." Could the schools serve the needs of the people by teaching a half hour each week? You say, "Impossible; our children would grow up in ignorance." Here we have a building which ought to be used every day, and many hours every week.

Both children and adults are growing up in ignorance of more important things than the schools are teaching. The brief amount of time our people spend at church is a shining example of this. Of the first century Christians, Acts 2:46, 47 says, "And they continued *daily* with one accord in the temple. . . . And the Lord added daily such as should be saved." We should have classes every afternoon and evening and see that our people are thoroughly grounded in the truth of God. Let us make use of our building!

A CHURCH BUILDING DEDICATION CEREMONY

The following scripture selections are suitable for reading on this occasion: Psa. 84:1-12; Psa. 100:1-5; 2 Chron. 29:15-19; Psa. 122.

Invocation:

"Behold, the tabernacle of God is with men, and he will dwell with them . . . and be their God" (Rev. 21:3).

"One thing have I desired of the Lord, that will I seek after; that I may dwell in the house of the Lord all the days of my life, to behold the beauty of the Lord, and to enquire in His temple" (Psa. 27:4).

Presentation of Keys to the Church:

Building committee representative hands keys to the minister and says,

I present to you, on behalf of the building committee, keys of this house, erected for the glory of God and the praise of His only begotten Son, Jesus our Lord and Saviour. May this house provide a home for this congregation where the ministry of the Word and all services of the church are carried on.

The Pastor Responds:

On behalf of this congregation and with sincere commendation to you and your committee for the splendid manner in which you have completed your task with the strong backing of this church, I accept this key in token of the high mission entrusted to us.

Pastor: Having been prospered by the good hand of the Lord and enabled by His grace and power to complete this house of worship, we will now in His holy presence dedicate the building to Him.

The People: Amen and Amen!

Pastor: Behold the tabernacle of God is with men and He shall dwell with them.

People: And they shall be His people and God Himself shall be their God.

Pastor: Who shall sojourn in the tabernacle?

People: Who shall abide in His holy Hill?

Pastor: He that hath clean hands and a pure heart.

People: He shall receive a blessing from the Lord and righteousness from the God of Jacob.

Pastor: Lift up your heads, O ye gates, lift them up ye everlasting hills, and the king of glory shall come in.

People: But will God dwell on the earth? Behold heaven and the heaven of heavens cannot contain Thee, how much less this house we have builded.

Pastor: Let the beauty of our God be upon us.

People: Yet we have respect, O Lord, unto the prayer which Thy servants pray before Thee this day, let Thine eyes be turned toward this house by day and by night.

Pastor: As the giving of the temple is in vain without the consecration of the people, we offer Thee our souls anew.

People: Through Thy Spirit dwell in our hearts, and may we be changed into Thy image from glory to glory.

Pastor: And so we bring Thee this place of assembly — this house we have builded.

People: We solemnly dedicate it to Thee!

Pastor: We set it apart for worship, for the sacrifices of broken hearts and contrite spirits.

People: For the reading of the Word of God, for the unfolding of the heavenly scroll, and the administration of the sacraments.

Pastor and People in Unison: Bow Thy heavens, O Lord, come down and make this Thy house now and forever Thy dwelling place. Fill it with Thy glory. Upon wall and window, upon lintel and doorpost, upon pulpit and pew, upon singers and orchestra, may there be written in letters of blood "holiness becometh thine house forever, O Lord."

People: Bless, we beseech, those who minister here. May they be fitted for the Master's use.

Pastor: And as they pray for strength, hear Thou in heaven Thy dwelling place and bless their ministry on earth to the souls of waiting people.

People: When tired, sin sick, hungry hearts come here with their need may they find the bread and water of life.

Pastor and People in Unison: We, the officers and people of this church and congregation do solemnly covenant together, to sacredly guard and uphold the doctrines and principles on which this church was founded. We will study the peace and unity of this church that it may ever serve for the assembling together of rich and poor for the worship of Him who is the maker of us all, and for the preaching of the Gospel in all its fulness and the uplifting of Jesus Christ as the only Saviour of men.

People: Here shall the incense of prayer and praise ascend to God, here shall the ordinances of the Lord's house be sacredly observed.

Pastor: Here shall the Word of God shine as a perpetual light to guide God's pilgrims through the night of time to the land of everlasting light.

People: Here shall the children of sin and sorrow find a refuge from sin and ruin, and Christians a harbor to which they can resort when the tempest is high and find safety.

Pastor: May no discordant note of strife ever be heard within these walls, no unholy spirit of pride or worldliness find entrance here.

People: May God accept this offering of an house in His Name — an offering made by grateful hearts and willing hands — and bless every heart that shares in this gift.

Pastor: May multitudes here be born to God, so that when all of us here today have gone to our eternal home, others will take up the work and carry it on till Jesus comes and all the redeemed are gathered home.

People: To the glory of God the Father, Son, and Holy Ghost, by whose favor we have builded, we dedicate this house. We, the sheep of His pasture, in joyful remembrance of our deliverance from the guilt and dominion of sin, do dedicate this house.

Pastor: Here let little children be taught the way of righteousness, the weak strengthened, the breaking heart consoled. Here manifest Thyself as a pardoning, consoling and comforting God to all who come to this house.

People: To the strong souls who stoop to share the burden of their fellows, to the weak and defenseless, to the darkened mind, the tempted heart, the weary and heavy laden, and to all human need, we dedicate this house.

Pastor: To our faithful missionaries laboring in heathen lands, to their support and encouragement, we dedicate this house.

People: To the memory of our beloved dead who tasted the cup of salvation in this place, but who have now gone to their reward to where the spirits of just men are made perfect, we dedicate this house.

Pastor: To the preservation of the family, the training and nurture of children, to the inspiration of youth, and to the salvation of all, we dedicate this house.

People: To the help of the needy, to the promotion of brotherhood, to the extension of His Kingdom throughout the whole wide world, we dedicate this house.

Pastor and People in Unison: Arise, O Lord, into Thy rest, and the ark of Thy strength. Let Thy ministers be clothed with righteousness, and let Thy people shout for joy. Let Thine eyes be opened toward this place, and harken to the supplications of Thy people when they pray in this place, and hear Thou in heaven Thy dwelling place, and when Thou hearest, forgive. Now establish Thou the work of our hands upon us, yea, the work of our hands establish Thou it. And to Thy blessed Name, O God, whose we are and whom we serve, be honor and glory everlasting, world without end, (*in unison*) Amen.

THE DEDICATION OF CHILDREN

The dedication of children is not generally practiced by the major denominations. It can be made a very effective service, however, and many parents never forget the vows made at the altar. These vows are a constant reminder of their obligations to the child, to God, and to the church. The service can be conducted in one of two ways, either in connection with another service, or a special one arranged for that purpose.

Some think the church should be decorated and this could well be but since this is a very sacred time to parents, the decorations should be limited and sacred in tone. If there is more than one family participating, children should be dedicated separately and not as a group. The dedication pledge should be administered to one family at a time. It will make the pledge more personal and impressive.

Suggested Order of Service:

(*After appropriate songs and reading of Scripture, a brief message similar to the following can be given*)

The coming of a new-born child brings joy. His life and presence brighten the home, making it more familylike. The home is no longer for a couple — a man and wife — but is now for a family. With the coming of a child there are larger responsibilities, not only for the upkeep of the child's physical welfare, but also for his spiritual welfare which is more important. This child has an immortal soul, the destiny of which depends to a great extent upon the Christian influence of the home. The scriptures give proof of this in the records of Hannah, Mary and Joseph, and the parents of Timothy. It would be a sad ending indeed, if this child should be brought up without the knowledge of God, and be lost in the end. Therefore, we come early in the child's life to dedicate it to the Lord while the parents acknowledge their responsibility and pledge themselves to bring it up in the nurture and admonition of the Lord.

(*The parents with the child or children to be dedicated are asked to come stand before the altar facing the minister, and the following pledge is administered*)

Do you, as parents of this child, understand that the vows you are about to take are binding before God as long as this child shall be under your care and government?

Answer: I do.

Will you, as parents chosen by God for this child, promise before God and this people that you will endeavor to bring this child up in the nurture and admonition of the Lord, that you will instruct it in the teachings of the Bible and the church? Will you do your best to see that you and your charge are in the house of God at the appointed time? Will you teach this child reverence for the church and its work? Will you instruct it in the way of holiness and live a life that will be an example for it to follow? Will you teach it to pray and show forth the worth of prayer and supplication before God? Will you seek to lead it to an early experience with God?

Answer: I will.

Then inasmuch as you have made this covenant with Almighty God and before His people, we now present this child to the Lord in dedication.

(Then the minister takes the child in his arms, if it is small, and lays his hands upon the larger ones. His prayer while holding the child is one of dedication.)

To you, the father of this child, I give this red flower as a symbol of the rich red blood with which you build and defend the home into which this child has come. Let nothing enter your home that will injure the soul of this child or crowd out the Lord who said, "Suffer the little children to come unto me and forbid them not for of such is the kingdom of heaven."

To the mother, I give this white flower as a symbol of the purity of heart with which you have endowed the home into which this child has come. If this child grows up to know God, it is likely to be because you have awakened its faith and nurtured it in the things of God. It is from you that the child gets its first ideas of God and the Saviour.

To the child I give this small white flower as a token of the innocency and purity of soul in the sight of God. My earnest prayer is that when you lose your innocency and the eyes of your understanding are opened, you will see Jesus, whom to see and know is eternal life.

Prayer:

Our Heavenly Father, we thank Thee for this service of dedication, and pray Thy blessing upon these parents and this child. May the child grow up to be a person after Thine own heart. May these parents be enabled by Thy Spirit to train and teach this child, that it may grow in wisdom and stature and in favor with God and with men. In Jesus' name we pray. Amen.

A SERVICE OF ORDINATION

Sermon at time of Ordination:

Scripture: 2 Tim. 2:19-26

It is a great day in the life of a church when a young man stands before a congregation to take the vows of the ministry. The church is to be congratulated, for it is sharing its young manhood with the brotherhood at large. The young man is to be congratulated, for he is enlisting full time in the service of the Lord.

For a number of years the young man Timothy had been Paul's helper. Then, in the midst of persecution, Paul is put in prison, and Timothy is left in charge of the work. Paul knows his days are numbered and he writes Timothy his final words of advice. His advice is treasured today and ought to be read by ministers constantly.

In as much as this young man has completed his preparation and is ready to launch out on his own, it is fitting that he, like Timothy, should be sent out with the words of Paul which will help him make full proof of his ministry.

1. Remember in becoming a minister you become not a dictator with absolute authority but a servant of the church. The laying on of hands does not confer authority on you, neither does it give you the gift of miracles. There will be many times when you will want miracles and wish you could do them, but remember miracles are the exception and not the rule. What the ministers do today is an act of approval and a sign of their unity with the body of believers. It is the church's way of saying it believes in you and recommends you to the churches everywhere as a worthy workman who can be depended upon to render a worthy service. You will be a leader and will present a definite program of work to the congregations you serve, or the mission field where you labor, but you will not force it on them.

2. In 1 Tim. 5:22 Paul says, "Keep thyself pure." This means in every way, both physically and spiritually. Be neat in your dress, clean in thought, and pure in heart. To be unclean not only is an insult to Jesus Christ, but it hurts the church and all religion. See that your conversation is above reproach. Paul said to Timothy, "Be not a partaker of other men's sins." For your own sake, as well as the bad impression it makes on others, keep your hands off women, old and young. Men distrust a man who is inclined to show familiarity with others' wives. You are beginning your work with a good character and you must always keep it that way. What you do will affect every life in the church and community.

3. *Be honest.* Many young preachers enter the ministry with no money and begin on a small salary or allowance, and then try to live on the same scale as the board members who have been working and saving for years. It can't be done, and debts are bound to increase. Whatever your salary may be, budget your income and live within it. It definitely hurts the church when word gets around town that the minister makes debts the merchants can not collect. You must be honest in every way.

4. *Prepare yourself as well as your sermons.* This is done by prayer

and communion with God. There is no substitute for it. It is a must. You have not prepared a sermon until you have prepared yourself. Prayer and waiting on God in the secret place give heart-power to the sermon. Without that, people will sense a "missing link" in your message. The punch and the move will not be there. This does not come easy. Here is where the price must be paid for results in the ministry. Some preachers deliver their sermons "crow fashion – two dips down and one look up." Remember people in distress need not mere preachers and speech makers; they need messengers from heaven, anointed with the Holy Ghost to bring a message that will cause men to tremble at His Word. Many people will never see you except on Sunday, and the impression they get of you on that day will stay with them. If you do not "carry the mail" that day, you will fail to have the respect and following of your congregation.

Be a Gospel preacher. People come to church to learn about God and the Bible. That is the time we have to work on the souls of men. They have heard politics and current events discussed all week, and now they are before you with hungry minds and hungry hearts.

Feed the flock. Don't try to be scholarly by throwing out a lot of Greek and Latin words that mean nothing to your listeners. People need to hear what they can understand.

Be positive in your preaching. Don't apologize for sharp, plain messages. The Word of God has always cut and burned. Use far more "do's" than "don't's." Seek always to build faith and deepen spirituality in the hearts of the people. Make the Gospel lively and so attractive that men will want to follow good instead of evil. Some preachers get a "drive" out of telling people off and "skinning" them, but be careful that once you have "skinned" them, you find you have failed to get enough out of their hides to pay your way out of town. You can refuse to compromise your message without being hateful. Jesus preached straight and the people flocked to Him. Be enthusiastic in the delivery of sermons. You have the greatest message in the world so give it gladly. This does not mean all shouting and pounding, as that usually means a preacher has run out of ideas. But it does mean there is no place for dull, lifeless sermons in a day when radio and television are bringing to people the finest kind of oratory. Always speak with conviction and sincerity.

5. *Make many calls on both members and prospects.* It is when you go to the homes that you render the finest service. It is when you call on people that they bring out their problems and ask

your advice. What you may miss in your sermons you gain in the homes. Let me caution you never to reveal what is told you in confidence. Your wife has no right to know the intimate problems of other people's lives. The law recognizes the personal nature of confidences and exempts ministers from repeating "privileged" conversations in court.

6. *Make the ordinances — the Lord's Supper and baptism — both beautiful and impressive.* Each of them carries a message that Christ died for our sins, and was buried and rose again. When you have a funeral service, make it helpful and comforting as it is conducted for the family and not the audience. God alone is the judge of the hearts and the condition of the souls of men. It is not for us to say who went to heaven and who went to hell. Let us try to go by what Paul says in 1 Tim. 4:16, "Take heed unto thyself, and unto the doctrine; continue in them; for in doing this thou shalt both save thyself, and them that hear thee."

Laying On of Hands:

Do you believe the Holy Scriptures of the Old and New Testaments to be Word of God, that they are the only rule of faith and practice, and that the Gospel of Jesus Christ is the power of God unto salvation to every one that believeth?

Answer: I do.

(*Candidate kneels and while the hands of the participating ministers are laid upon him, the following prayer may be offered:*)

"Our Father, from the beginning Thou hast sent men to carry Thy Word into all the world. Thou hast sent into Thy Vineyard men as apostles, evangelists, pastors and teachers. We beseech Thee to grant Thy gifts of grace and power, of prophetic zeal and apostolic fire to this Thy servant, that through him Thy Word may be effectively and faithfully preached, Thy Name magnified, and many souls brought to Thee and built up in the most Holy Faith. We ask it in Jesus' Name. Amen.

Presentation of Bible:

(*The minister hands the ordained a Bible*)

Take now this Bible of which you are appointed an interpreter Be diligent to "study to show thyself approved unto God." Take this Word into your own heart so that you may proclaim it with warmth, conviction and power. To the limit of your understanding and ability, faithfully preach the gospel of the grace of God. Be yourself an example of faith and devoted living so that no one in following you will stumble or fall and be lost to the Kingdom of God or His church.

Charge to the Candidate:

We remind you that from this day there is no turning back from the choice you have made and the way you have chosen.

The vows of God are now on you! Your hands have gripped the Gospel plow, and we charge you never to let go regardless of the high cost of your consecration to the office of the holy ministry. We charge you to be a faithful and loving shepherd to the sheep and not to neglect to care for the lambs. Our prayers are with you that you shall be strengthened when you are weak, guided when the way is not clear, and that Christ shall be your companion when you are lonely. We also pray that you will be made helpful to your "yoke-fellows" in the ministry, and that you will always remember that you are God's servant ordained to the office of the ministry by the laying on of the hands.

I charge thee therefore before God and the Lord Jesus Christ, who shall judge the quick and the dead at His appearing and His kingdom, Preach the Word; be instant in season and out of season, reprove, rebuke, exhort with all longsuffering and doctrine; and when the Chief Shepherd shall appear, you shall receive a crown of glory that fadeth not away.

(Here participating ministers extend the right hand of fellowship to the one ordained with these or similar words, "I give you the right hand of fellowship in token of your acceptance into the fellowship of the Gospel).

A Prayer by the One Ordained (To be prayed in private):

Lord, I am not worthy that Thou shouldest come under my roof, but since Thou hast called me to preach Thy Word and to administer the ordinances of Thy house, help me to cause men to see that Thy Son Jesus Christ came into this world to make clear Thy image and show us all the way of salvation. Thou hast sent prophets, evangelists and ministers to carry the message of redeeming love. Lord, Thou and these men who have laid hands upon me have set me apart to proclaim Thy Word, to administer the sacraments, and to nurture Thy people. Bestow Thy benediction upon me, place Thy hand upon me, and ordain me to preach the Gospel in the Name of the Father, the Son and the Holy Ghost. Send Thy Holy Spirit upon me and awaken me to see the might that is in Thine arm. Anoint me to preach the Gospel to the poor, to heal the brokenhearted, to preach deliverance to the captives and the recovery of sight to the blind, and to set at liberty those who are captive. Surround me with Thy hallowed presence. Send me forth to do Thy will. May I keep Thy Word and never deny Thy Name. In the Name of Christ our Lord. Amen.

A SERVICE FOR THE ORDINANCE OF WATER BAPTISM

(For Believers' Baptism by Immersion)

"And he took them the same hour of the night, and washed their stripes; and was baptized, he and all his straightway" (Acts 16:33).

All Christians are impressed with the beauty and significance of the believer's baptism in water. When people are first saved from sin, they are so overjoyed and thrilled with the presence of Jesus in their hearts they do not hesitate to obey this command to be baptized. Indeed they are eager to pass through this simple outward rite which expresses their desire to follow Christ all the way.

First, *the person to be baptized must be a believer,* one who believes in the Lord Jesus Christ. We sometimes hear people speak of "adult baptism." This is a misleading statement. If one is as old as Methuselah but does not believe, he has no right to be baptized; while any child who trusts in the Saviour has the right of baptism. Christ did not ask for emotional upheavals, visions or exuberance, or maturity of years. He only asked faith, "He that believeth and is baptized shall be saved" (Mark 16:16).

Second, *the mode of baptism.* It must be by immersion. That is, dipping the whole body beneath the water. If there were no other argument to prove that this was the ancient and scriptural mode, the question would be settled for us by an appeal to Romans 6. The whole point of the argument there is this: The waters of baptism are a grave; baptism is a burial; the baptized one is buried into the likeness of Christ's death. Joseph and Nicodemus bore the lifeless body of the Lord to burial in the garden tomb where it was hid from the sight of men. What likeness can baptism have to the resurrection of Christ, unless the whole body can be lifted from the grave-like waters into the upper air and light? No wonder John baptized in a certain place "because there was much water there" (John 3:23). A good supply of water was always on hand in Jerusalem for the use of the priests and for temple purposes, otherwise the three thousand new converts could not have been baptized in one day (Acts 2:41).

Third, *believers' baptism is binding on Christians* for the following reasons. (1) *Our Lord was baptized.* When He was thirty, He mixed with the crowds that thronged the banks of the Jordan and asked baptism at the hands of John the Baptist. He that baptizes with the Holy Ghost and fire was Himself baptized with water (Matt. 3:13; John 1:33). This should be reason enough why all should be.

(2) *Christ commanded baptism by saying,* "Go ye and teach all nations, baptizing them . . ." (Matt. 28:19). These words are the marching orders of the church. We are not at liberty to alter or question them; we must simply obey. If we could not see any meaning to the ordinance, we should still submit to it anyway, because He commanded it. It is not enough to talk love; let us show it by obedience. The apostles practiced it. Wherever they went, they used the rivers and reservoirs for this holy rite. They practiced it in Jerusalem (Acts 2:41), in Samaria (Acts 8:12), in the desert (Acts 8:36), among the Gentiles, in the house of the soldier Cornelius, and in the prison of the jailer at Philippi (Acts 10:48; 16:33).

Fourth, *baptism is the symbol of the forgiveness of sins.* "They were baptized of him confessing their sins" (Matt. 3:6). This original meaning of baptism remains. Sin is constantly described as a stain; forgiveness is spoken of as a washing white — whiter than the driven snow.

Fifth, *baptism is a mark of discipleship.* This is the meaning especially attached to it by Christ himself, "Go ye and make disciples of all nations, baptizing them." The Lord looked around for some universal act which should serve as a badge of His disciples and there was nothing so suitable as baptism.

Sixth, *it marks a break with the old and a start for a new life.* Christ's burial broke His earthly life into two parts. He was different on this side of the grave from what He was on the other. Physical weakness was replaced by resurrection life; dishonor by glory; weakness by power; a natural body by a spiritual body (1 Cor. 15:43). Something like this happens when a man comes to Christ. He dies and is buried to his old sinful past. He rises into the strength of Christ, into a new and glorious life. Now it is well to have an outward sign to impress all this on believers and on the world, and the Holy Ghost led the Apostles to put this new meaning into baptism. "Know ye not, that so many of us as were baptized into Jesus Christ, were baptized into his death? Therefore we are buried with him by baptism unto death: that like as Christ was raised up from the dead by the glory of the Father, even so we also should walk in newness of life" (Rom. 6:3, 4). Then when we are baptized, we proclaim our faith in certain distinct facts: that Christ once lived upon our earth in human flesh; that He died for our sins according to the scriptures; that He was buried and arose again on the third day; that He is living still; and that His Word is law and we as His followers bow to it. We should keep all the Lord's wishes because obedience makes a big difference in our enjoyment of His presence. If we love Him, we will keep His commandments.

PART II

HELPS FOR SPECIAL DAYS

NEW YEAR'S DAY

"Set your affections on things above, not on things on the earth" (Col. 3:2).

The old year is behind us. We cannot change it. Doubtless there is much in it we would like to change, some things we are ashamed of, and some things left undone which we regret; but the page is turned, the year is gone to shame or to blame us as the case may be. The new year is before us. Its dawn has just come up out of the radiant east. Its record is yet to be made. It is within our power to determine what it shall be.

We are at the top line of the first page. What sort of a start shall we make? Here is my message.

Make a grand new start! How can this be done? Darkness and gloom come from turning to the arm of flesh. Cheer and brightness come from turning for a new look at the promises of God. There are those people who always insist on blowing out the light to see how dark it is. Remember, strength and light come from the hills of God, not from traveling companions. Our generation is full of problems, but God has not deserted us. This world of ours has been in business a long time.

The course of human history is never smooth or even. The year 1810 was said by many writers of that time to be the "twilight of the race." It was midway between the battle of Trafalgar and Waterloo, and even in that dark hour, God's forces were working in ways that people knew nothing about. At that very time there was a lad named Abraham Lincoln playing before the doorway of his mother's cabin in the Kentucky mountains; Alfred Tennyson, the poet-prophet of the English race, was just beginning to dream his dreams; and Oliver Holmes was a babe in his mother's arms. In the world's darkest hours God has matched the evil of men with new life and power.

Let us take a long look into the new year. The long look gives us faith in a God big enough to be worthy of our worship. We need to humble ourselves anew before His majesty and power.

A new start should be a straight start—not just to do well, or as good as others, but to beat your best! You will hear plenty of uncomplimentary remarks about new year's resolutions. Some will say they do not amount to much, that they are soon broken, and that people who break them turn out like the man Jesus told about whose last state was worse than the first. Don't take this kind of talk too seriously. There is a bigger and better crowd cheering you on! Paul says in Heb. 12:1, that we are compassed about by a great cloud of witnesses. If just one keeps on, the custom is redeemed.

Winston Churchill once wrote a book entitled *Their Finest Hour*. That book had to do with bearing hardships in time of war. But we Christians are in a war of a different kind. It is a "fine hour" when the best stirs you to come to a summit on life's rough road, when you are lifted to a glimpse of the shoreline of heaven, when you hear a song, or when you see the face of a friend that sends determination surging to the front until you make a new resolution, saying, "I will shake off my shabby habits, crucify my lusts, kick the filth from my mind, snap the shackles and be free!" I am sorry for the man who never has such an hour, who never climbs a peak, who never feels an ecstasy, who never has a thrill, but who just trudges along with his head down, his pulses dull and his senses stale. What if a man does go up like a rocket and comes down like a stick. His heart was not wrong. No step in the right direction is ever lost! The recording angel writes down not only every good deed but every brave start, and it is all on the credit side. Nothing good ever perishes. Every sob of pity that ever broke over a desolate heart and every breath of prayer directed to Heaven is somewhere, for it can never die. A good start contributes to a grand continuing. A car gathers momentum as it moves, and less power is needed to keep going than is required to start. We have all learned that cars have to be started in low gear, but a car in motion helps move itself. It is the same with life. A life motion helps itself. If the start is wrong, it is easier to go wrong; if right, it is easier to go right.

Help is to be had. God who starts us stays with us. A soul in action is not deserted by the Saviour. Let's make this the day when we move out! If you want to feel Heaven astir in your soul, get moving! Burn the bridges behind you. Jesus said that whosoever putteth his hand to the plough and looketh back is not fit for the kingdom of God (Luke 9:62). These back-lookers are in bad business. They soon become backsliders.

God sees the motive. It is not how high you climb but how hard you struggle. People travel the road of life with different handicaps, and these must be taken into account in estimating one's record. God's promise is "To him that overcometh," not to him that maketh a mile a minute, that crosses a goal line first, that makes a new speed record, but "To him that overcometh shall be given the crown." It is not how many victories you win, but how desperately you fight your battles. There is no such thing as defeat for a soldier who dies fighting for his cause. Motive is the big thing with God.

Set your affections on things above. People follow their hearts. What men love they go after. May your treasures be in Heaven. You will climb toward them. Observe the words of the text: God does not "set your affections"; you set them yourselves. You can go to the mourner's bench and ask your brothers and sisters to pray that your affections will be set right, but do it yourself. You can associate with people who will either lift you up or drag you down. You have will power. You control your optic nerve. You can let your eyes gaze on the best in life, or let them gaze on sights that fan flames that slumber in your flesh. Where are your pleasures located — in your brains or heels, in your head or feet? Today, for a grand new beginning, "set your affections on things above." If you have a habit that is dragging you to hell, a new start means kicking that habit. You may imagine the habit has hold of you, but how did it ever get hold of you? Now let go even if you have to break a bone to loosen your grip and be free. There are some who are just beginning to nibble at the naughty side of life. You may not know the devil's bait when you see it. That is the way all ruin starts. Every soul in hell began by playing with fire. A good beginning means to quit! Jesus is the Alpha and the Omega, the beginning and the ending, and it is those who start in Him and run well that take the crown.

GOOD FRIDAY

"He Went a Little Further"

"And he took with him Peter and the two sons of Zebedee, and began to be sorrowful and very heavy. Then saith he unto them, My soul is exceedingly sorrowful, even unto death: tarry ye here, and watch with me. And he went a little further, and fell on his face, and prayed, saying, O my Father, if it be possible, let this cup pass from me: nevertheless not as I will, but as thou wilt" (Matt. 26:37-39). This is one of great texts of the Bible, and like many others, there is a message in it for everyone. Were each one to stop reading after hearing this text, he would carry a life changing message with nothing more added.

There is something here for my heart and also yours. There is not a life that would not be better, happier, and more useful, if one would do what Jesus did in this lesson; namely, "go a little further." If every man in this house who is not a Christian would do this, not one would leave the building unsaved. If I know my own heart at this hour I want to go a little further, and I trust it is the determination of everyone present.

My heart saddens when I think of so many who do not take this step, and therefore are living miserable and fruitless lives. They lack the last step. They have gone so far, but they need to go a little further. If Satan can keep a man from going a little further, he will keep the Christian out of a blessing and the sinner out of heaven. Christian, if you are not close to Jesus today, move up a little closer, go a little further; you cannot go too far in that direction. To the unsaved, you who have a burdened heart and a load of guilt that presses down upon you like a mountain, let me tell you that you are near the fountain filled with blood. This fountain washes away sin and guilt. Will you move up a little further?

The step means life or death. Today you have a choosing hour, a great hour! What will you do with it? Some soul will enter the gateway of blessing while others will move further away.

Witness a touching scene. For days the shadow of the cross had been deepening upon the pathway of our blessed Lord. When He took the lonely step referred to in this passage, He was going where no other soul had ever gone! He was going where no other soul can ever go this side of the grave. He was going to be God-forsaken. He saw it all when He entered Gethsemane. That is why I think He went alone.

The intimate disciples, Peter, James, and John, could not follow Him there. He had just said to the Jews that where He would go they could not follow Him (John 13:33). He left eight of them at the gate. He took the three a little further, and then He left them to watch while in the night He moved away about a stone's throw.

If He had not gone a little further, you and I would never have been redeemed. The distance between Christ and the disciples was short, but they were poles apart in spirit. They were sleeping, and He was agonizing. They were thinking of thrones, and He was thinking of the cross and thorns! They were to receive salvation, but He was to bleed to obtain it.

Yes, the distance could be walked in a few minutes, but measured by the line of spiritual experience, it was a great gulf. Let us think of the loneliness of which these words remind us. He had left for the last time the home of Mary and Martha. His body had now been anointed for burial. He carries the sentence of death within Him. He had broken the bread at the last supper and said "Remember me." He had taken a look at the disciples He loved and knew they would soon forsake Him and flee. Judas was downtown arranging for His betrayal. He and the mob would soon be coming. He was sore troubled. Now He felt God withdrawing. Midnight was piling on midnight. That was all beginning in the heart of Jesus when He went a little further.

Where did those tears begin to fall and that blood to flow? Not on the cross, but in Gethsemane! There He felt the cross before He came to it. His was a long journey. He had carried the cross in His heart from eternity. He was a "lamb slain from the foundation of the world." There He not only tasted the cup of our bitter woe, but He drained it to the dregs. No wonder He groaned as He saw the flood of our sin and guilt coming on. It was not on the cross but in Gethsemane's garden that the strong cryings ascended and the hot tears fell, but "He went a little further." He trod the winepress alone and of all the people there was none with Him.

This was part of the price of man's redemption. Unless Christ took that step, that last step, that awful step, you and I would have perished forever; but He moved on into that awful shadow, through which the light of heaven did not penetrate, until He reached the other side of the cross. Jesus stood firm in His determination to pay the uttermost farthing for our redemption.

Martin Luther said, "Here I stand—I cannot recant! God help me!" Some have stood, others wilted and failed. Let us glance at some examples from the Word of God. God said to Saul, "Slay all—everything." He failed, kept the best of the herds and flocks, and lost his crown. Ten cowardly spies spread gloom over the nation and they failed. A "little further" would have meant Canaan. Take the case of Herod. "A little further" would have saved his soul. He kept his brother's wife and perished. Felix "trembled" but didn't repent. Agrippa was convinced he needed Christ, and said, "Almost thou persuadest me to be a Christian." In that moment think what a "further" step would have done for him! The rich young ruler or the lawyer who was not far from the kingdom of God had the bundle at their finger tips, but went the other way "sorrowfully." Pilate had his big chance to save his soul and future but refused to take the step and yielded to the clamor of the mob.

This world is poor without Jesus! Is there anyone who can take His place? In life? In death? In judgment? None. In the parable of the Pearl, the man "sold all and bought it." There is nothing worth keeping at the price of losing Christ and our souls. Go "a little further" and you will find God and salvation, peace and a new life, and heaven at last. Yes, there is a Gethsemane for every man and woman; a place where each surrenders fully to the will of God, and takes up the prayer Jesus prayed, "Father, not my will but thine be done." No man can pray these words until he is a Christian.

"The battle of life is won,
And heaven begun,
When we can say thy will be done,
But Lord until these restless hearts,
In thy deep love are still,
O teach us how to do thy will."

The last step involves a recognition of the fact that Christ alone can save. That is hard for men to do. They want a hand in their salvation. But God's way is still, "Nothing in my hands I bring, simply to thy cross I cling." The last step means a complete break with sin and the old life and the crowd and the old things. Any move of yours that leaves you in sin is not big enough to save you. You can have conviction, and promise to do better. Take the "old man of sin" by the hair of the head or the nape of the neck and cast him out for keeps. Confess Christ openly. There is no smuggling into the kingdom of heaven. The woman you read about in the Gospels that "touched the hem of his garment" from behind, had to come to the front and openly own Him. Why not confess Him now?

EASTER

"He is not here, but is risen: remember how he spake unto you when he was yet in Galilee, saying, The Son of man must be delivered into the hands of sinful men, and be crucified, and the third day rise again" (Luke 24:6-7). The darkest picture this old war-scarred, sin-cursed world ever saw was Golgotha's cross. The very heavens bowed themselves in midnight mourning and wept. The flinty rocks—more yielding than many hearts I know—burst in their dumb grief because their Maker was put to death by the hands of those He came to save and bless. And if the seal that was placed on the tomb of Joseph of Arimathaea had remained unbroken, death would have been to us an endless sleep. But now is Christ risen from the dead and become the firstfruits of them that are sleeping; and because He lives, we shall live also.

Earth's most famous shrines where pilgrims go are the spots which hold the ashes of great mortals whom men have loved, revered and often worshipped because the honored dead are there. Countless Americans, including this speaker, have journeyed down the Potomac River from Washington to Mount Vernon, Virginia, to the home of George Washington. The hours spent there were crowded with interest and emotion because of the memories that dwell in the place where lived the man who guided and safeguarded our country's government. But the chief emotion and deepest reverence focuses upon the simple tomb. Why? Because all that is mortal of the nation's founder is "there." In the heart of the Andes mountains of Peru once lived the Sunworshippers, people who had splendid engineers and stone cutters to terrace stairways into the side of the mountains where they placed their dead. For one thousand years they made pilgrimages to this spot. Why? Because their dead were there. Yearly the emperor of Japan makes a pilgrimage, attended by royal princes, to worship at the grave of his imperial ancestors. The earliest historic emperors were buried there and they believe their spirits are still there so they take them food, wine and perfumes and offer prayers to them. Why? Because their dead are there.

This practice was very pronounced in Egypt. Thebes, their ancient capital, was known as the city of one hundred gates that ruled the world. From there you may go up the Nile to the Valley of the Dead. It is empty of every living thing. There the Pharaohs drove shafts in the heart of the mountains and hewed out secret galleries, then mummified their bodies so they could rest there from age to age. Men who controlled the then civilized world are there among the dead. In Rome, Italy, they have the Appian Way (the Apostle Paul came over this road when he entered Rome as a prisoner) which was an avenue of the princely dead. Over this road the Mistress of the world took her nobles, generals, and Caesars, and over them reared marble memorials. The marbles have been stolen or are crumbling, the walls are falling in, but the dead of Rome are there.

The English race has one Westminster Abbey, where kings have been crowned and kings have been buried. The dead whom the nation delighted to honor — warriors, dreamers, statesmen, missionaries, painters, singers — the noble, the loved. The whole Commonwealth is fascinated by Westminster because its dead are there.

You may belt the globe or cover the six continents of the world, and you find famous shrines attracting pilgrims. But add to this the trackless roadways of the seven seas that have swallowed and hidden deep the dead of the ages. The floors of the seas are populated. The dead are there.

We live but a brief term of years; in one century three generations enter the grave. In one hundred years earth has three new outfittings of humanity, who inhabit the earth, use it, then go to rest in it. For many generations, the tombs have been filling until the cities of the dead outnumber a thousand fold the cities of the living. There is no spot to be found but what you are compelled to say, "The dead are there." Think how those still narrow houses of the graves multiply in our day. Europe had ten million freshly made graves — the harvest of one single war. How hastily earth's cities of death have widened their boundaries to receive the old and young of all races of mankind.

Go back to the first maze of death and remember Cain and Seth burying their father and ours, Adam, the man who should have been immortal, who had the right to eat of the tree of life and live forever, but sinned and died; and since that time men have been gathered to their fathers. This fate of death was shared by three men, who, on one Passover feast, died at Jerusalem on the hill of execution just outside the city wall, under sentence of the Roman governor, Pilate.

But, strangely, two members of the Jewish supreme court took down the body of one of the dead from His cross and placed it in a new tomb in a private garden near Calvary. Watched by weeping women, they closed the door of that tomb just as millions of tomb doors have been closed in all ages. That tomb was occupied. Men knew the dead was there, just as in every other tomb in all the vaults of time. The next day a Roman officer came with the governor's seal and affixed it to the tomb door. By this the power of Rome guaranteed that the dead in that tomb must stay there. Death was the penalty to anyone who should break the seal or take away the dead. So Joseph's tomb joined the multitude of tombs in all ages that held the dead.

Then a new dawn breaks and a new light comes into Joseph's new tomb. A white messenger came and spoke words that were never before spoken in any of mankind's tombs — this word: "He is not here." None of the burying places on the six continents of the world heard the words spoken that morning by the angel. Mourning women were frightened and speechless. His closest friends marvelled and disbelieved. How could the rule of death be broken? The angel said, "He is risen." The faith of the church throughout the centuries has been that Christ rose from the dead as the firstfruits from the dead, and has entered as our pattern and forerunner into mansions of greater glory prepared for Him and for us all. "Because I live, ye shall live also," He said. Firstfruits foretell a complete harvest to follow. We are the harvest; we, the dead, that have inhabited the tombs of the ages; we, the dead shall awaken! We shall join Him and share in His triumph.

Let us look to another miracle morning — not too distant, or near! It will be at dawn again, I think, when light is reborn after night! I imagine that it will be a spring morning, sparkling with dew, when life returns out of this earth, when creation itself "also shall be delivered from the bondage of corruption into the glorious liberty of the children of God" (Rom. 8:21). On that new greatest Easter morning, every tomb of every believer in every land shall be opened at the dawn, as Joseph's was, by the same Almighty power. And over every tomb and the flashing waves of the seven seas, the resurrection angel shall stand again, and shall say to us the same words, "He is not here. He is up here in the air." Those places that have known the dead shall know them no more. This is the certain faith of the believer; this is the great hope of the Easter morning.

MOTHER'S DAY

"Thy mother" (2 Tim. 1:5).

In 1908, Miss Anna Jarvis, of Philadelphia, Pennsylvania, observed the first "Mother's Day" in memory of her own mother. Believing others shared her feelings, she began a nationwide movement to have the day observed. She struck a responsive chord in nearly every heart. Little by little the idea grew. The Congress of the United States set apart the day by a formal act, and the President recommended its observance. It is now not only a national day but international. Country after country has responded to its appeal until its observance on the second Sunday in May each year has become world-wide.

Well may we pause to honor her, who after Jesus Christ, is God's best gift to men — Mother. It was she who went down into the valley of the shadow of death to usher her children through the gates of life. In her arms was the garner of food and the soft couch for our sleep. There we nestled in the hour of pain; there was the playground of our infant glee. Those same arms later became our refuge and stronghold. It was she who taught our baby feet to go and lifted us over the rough places. Her hands plied the needle by day and night to make the little garments we should wear. She put the book under our arms and started us off to school. Best of all she taught our baby lips to lisp the name of Jesus and told us first the story of His love.

Perhaps she lives to bless your life. Maybe the silver crowns her temples, and your children call her grandmother. It may now be your turn to minister to her at eventide. Bless God for the privilege. Plant the grateful kiss on her face and send her the message of your love. If she has been called up higher to join the blood-washed throngs in the presence of the Lamb, then wear the white flower in memory of her and foster the sentiment of "Mother's Day."

When Jesus would teach the great truths of God's providence and care, He said, "Consider the lilies" – God will take care of you. Let the white carnation, emblem of Mother's Day, bring us to its message of motherhood. Its whiteness tells of purity, its form of beauty, its fragrance of love, its wide field of growth tells of charity, and its lasting qualities of faithfulness. Motherhood does not count itself to have attained perfection, yet it is the choicest flower of earthly affection and most like the love of God. The white carnation is its fitting emblem.

One. Its whiteness tells us of the purity of motherhood. God pity the misguided soul that vainly thinks himself superior to others because of a life of celibacy! He hides behind the wall of hypocrisy to sling mud at the one who bore him! Wedlock is holy, and "forbidding to marry" is one of the marks of decay in the last days (1 Tim. 4:3). But even God's holy ordinance of matrimony may be perverted into legalized vice. Love that belongs to a baby should never be lavished on a brindle pup!

It is true there are wicked mothers like Jezebel of old. There are sin-soaked, rum-scarred mothers to whom their motherhood is an exposure of their shame. I am glad to believe there are few in this class.

Two. No man loves his mother as he ought who does not stand up to the protection of womanhood everywhere and under all circumstances. Last year 70,000 girls in America were lost to decent living, never to appear on the stage of virtuous action again. This should be a call to men to rise up and crush out this nefarious traffic in blood and souls. Every true man must set himself against this traffic, which, if not arrested would make "Mother's Day" an impossible farce.

Appeals must be made to the strong arm of the law to punish those who lead away silly women like sheep to the shambles and to put about our girls such protection as they have a right to expect. The vast majority of those who turn aside from the path of virtue are illiterate, cannot write their names. This makes them an easy prey for desiring men and women. Education is only one of the remedies. First and basic is the new birth of the power of the Word of God and the Spirit and then faithful moral training in the homes. Public schools, theatres and dance halls are no place for children to learn their lessons in morals, but in the atmosphere of the home with mother as the teacher.

Three. Not all mothers are beautiful. Though your mother is beautiful to you, not all women are favored with symmetry of face and form; but all motherhood is beautiful. The hen with her brood attracts attention; the mother cow with her calf is an object of interest; how much more the human mother and her babe. The greatest picture in the world is the Madonna and her Child. The charm of it never grows old. Peep into that Christian home at twilight. There in the glow of the open fire is the mother with her babe. She is crooning lullabies interspersed with broken baby talk and the little cherub (as he is to his mother) answers with a coo and a sputter, which is full compensation to the mother for all her efforts. Christ says in Matt. 18:10, "That in heaven their angels do always behold the face of my Father which is in heaven." Yes, into these mother hands God has entrusted a budding mortality and to her is committed the sacred task of making the first impressions upon the tablets of the child-heart.

Four. There is a similarity between the carnation and the mother. The family tree of the carnation is famous. It is the "cloves" tree of the tropics. It produces aromatic spices, it bears fruit to eat, and its oil is a medicine. With such a family record the carnation makes an atmosphere all its own. When bruised or cut it breathes on to bless others.

In joy or sorrow, laughter or tears, that perfume exhales its fragrance to bless all who come within the circle of its influence. There is no influence so potent in forming character as that of a mother. In many cases she is weaving the coat of character the child will wear forever!

The motherless boy hasn't had a fair chance in the world; he has run the race with a handicap. Great men have usually owed their achievements to their mothers. Lincoln said, "All I am and ever hope to be, I owe to my angel mother." But the motherless boy or, worse still, the boy with a worthless mother, is to be pitied. When a worthless son of a worthless mother on his way to prison, asked to speak to his mother and, instead, bit off her ear, he was not altogether to be blamed. She had robbed him of his birthright!

No nation is greater than its mothers. They are makers of men. When Greece and Rome had mothers to train their children they stood without rivals; but when Greece produced a crop of perfumed dandies and Rome her jeweled debauchees like Otho and Nero, God began to wipe out their glory, and today they are a mere shadow.

Five. We have all heard of the son of a widowed mother who graduated from the University with honors and at the commencement when the gold medal was handed him he walked to the back of the room where his mother sat by the door in a black dress. He placed the medal around her neck. The great throng cheered and cheered. The son was remembering how she labored and toiled to keep him in school. But every true mother knows the honors should not rest with her. She lays her trophies at the feet of the Lord Jesus who was Mary's great Son. In honoring our mothers our hearts are lifted into the worship and praise of our mother's God.

BACCALAUREATE

Scripture: Matt. 13:46

Today you step out into a world of reality. You have been taught that your ancestors were great people. You have been told of their achievements after a discouraging start. Although they were a part of a small world, you are a part of a big and changing one. You have been told your ancestors held a mortgage on all good principles, and their sons have been foreclosing them ever since. It is good for you to know the rugged and sturdy stock from which you have come. Your forefathers subdued the forests, organized emigration, marched westward as soldiers of the pioneers, they figured in the founding of Concord and Lexington, Paul Revere's Ride, the Charter Oak, Harvard and Yale. They preserved the Union, annihilated slavery, made the promises of the nation equal to gold.

You are going out into a country of approximately two hundred million. You could easily accept the idea that the individual doesn't count, and that he or she might as well go with the tide. It is for you to decide if you will be buried in this bundle of humanity and lost in the shuffle. There are certain things you can do that will give your personality a "cutting edge", that will make you a stand-out. The purpose of this institution has been to assist you in preparing for the future, to help discover your talents and teach you how to use them. Do not miss this message. Let me warn you there are forces of sin and evil working in this great world of ours. Some of these are open and some are hidden. It is my place to uncover and show their hiding places.

One of your problems will be *mastery of self*. Right here it is well to be reminded of what the Bible says in Prov. 16:32, "He that ruleth his own spirit is greater than he that taketh a city." Much history in the old world is connected with Alexander the Great. Let us take a look at his background. When Alexander was a boy, his father had a beautiful but vicious horse which could not be broken and he was ready to sell him. Alexander begged that he might have the horse. He noticed the animal was afraid of his shadow. Alexander mounted him and turned his face to the sun and made him run until he was exhausted. Daily he repeated this until he was under complete control. At the age of sixteen, his father turned over the regency of Greece to him. At twenty-one, he had destroyed Thebes; at twenty-five, he had conquered Babylonia; and at thirty three he had subdued the civilized world. He learned to tame animals and nations, but he never learned how to master himself. He died a drunkard without ever doing anything really useful in the world. Self-mastery is one of the pressing problems young people must solve. You must learn that other people have rights, and that they must be respected, and that you cannot always have your way.

Great athletes know the value of self-mastery. They neither drink nor smoke. They eat the right food, get proper sleep, and learn to work with others. They study the rules and struggle when the odds are against them.

The problem of friends. It is natural to want them, but you have to do something to get them and to keep them. Solomon said, "He that hath friends must show himself friendly" (Prov. 18:24). That is to say, you cannot be hateful and critical and still be surrounded by friends. You can do a few things that will help. Make use of compliments when you can honestly do so. They cost you nothing but are precious to others. Make others feel important instead of inferior. Ask their advice. Get them to talk about themselves. They will think you are the Prince of Wales or the Queen of Sheba. Remember you never win friends by winning arguments. If you have to disagree with others, be nice about it

Finding life's work. Many of you are eager to get out of school, make money and get married. You can do that, but in life you never find the fullest measure of happiness until you find the work you are particularly fitted for. You may have talents buried in your soul that need to be dug up, developed and put to work. Don't be satisfied doing something easy on the surface but bring to light those qualities within your life of greatest worth and they will give you abiding satisfaction.

I think it fitting to relate again how the California Gold Rush was started. In 1845 two brothers came to this country from Europe. One knew how to make sauerkraut and the other had no trade. The kraut maker joined a wagon train going west. After arriving in California, he started raising cabbage. The younger boy went to school and studied metallurgy. One day he went to California to see his brother, who showed him his fine cabbage patch. In the course of the tour, the boy was looking at the stones on the ground. He saw a stone with a yellow spot on it. The older boy was offended because the younger boy took no interest in his cabbage. The metallurgist said, "Do you know what that yellow spot is? That's gold." They took it to the laboratory and had it examined. It was gold. The younger boy said, "You have been raising cabbage on a gold field." That was the beginning of the richest gold strike in the West. The California Gold Rush followed. You might be found doing the same thing.

Religion. Christ said, "Seek ye first the kingdom of God and his righteousness and all these things shall be added unto you" (Matt. 6:33).

Our quest for the best ends when we find God. Do not be afraid nor ashamed to speak of Him and serve Him. You are living in God's world and it is a good one. You breathe His air and eat His food. He keeps your heart beating day and night. He gives you a body in which to live and a mind with which to think and a soul with which to love. You owe Him more than you can ever repay.

Young people, do not wait until you are about to die to think of God. Life has a beginning and an ending. There are three stages in life: youth, manhood and old age. It is said youth is a blunder, manhood a struggle and old age a regret, but the ideal is: youth is opportunity, manhood is achievement and old age is a holy memory.

There are some things necessary for getting the best in life:

Begin with Christ: "Remember now thy Creator in the days of thy youth" (Eccles. 12:1). Take Him as your soul's partner. Put Him first. He needs helpers and partners. He needs you. Whatever vocation you choose, count Him in. You need real conviction. That gives you stability. It makes you strong in purpose, firm in resolution. A conviction founded upon the Word of God gives you ground to stand on. When you know you are in the right place, no power can turn you away from it. Such a man cannot fail. Let the Bible be your guide. It is the best for this life and the life to come. It is God's map to guide us through life. With it you can tread your way through all winding paths of life with perfect safety. So many young people go out to face the world of sin and darkness with no knowledge of God's Word. This is a terrific mistake. What a tragedy! They are exposed to all the wiles of the devil. David said, "Thy word is a lamp to my feet and a light to my path."

Have a few friends among the old folks. They have been where you are and you will soon be where they are. They are acquainted with the rough places in the road.

Meet the frowning world with a smile. Smiles never go up in price nor down in value. It takes the oil of kindness to run the machinery of life.

You may have long and strenuous hours of toil, but you will reach your goal. It takes energy to make life count for the best.

Abraham Lincoln fought his way through his difficulties by working like a giant. He cut logs to build a cabin. He studied law by the firelight. He never gave up and became the sixteenth President of the United States. Some begin with wealth and go to the bottom. He began in poverty and went to the top.

Heavenly Father: We give thanks to Thee for the blessings Thou hast sent upon our land. While other lands have remained in darkness and superstition, America has had light in its dwellings. From the beginning the light, freedom and opportunity have guided our feet. We have been protected from hazards and pestilences and Thou hast fulfilled Thy promise to us "that no evil shall befall thee and no plague shall come nigh thy dwelling." As we recall all these things and the fact they come from Thee, may we be an humble and grateful people. Our forefathers have bequeathed to us an heritage we cherish and trust we shall be able to pass on to others. Truly the words of Christ are fulfilled tonight that, "Other men have labored and we have entered in their labors." We thank Thee for our schools with their great education and cultural advantages, for this student body and the staff who have faithfully worked to prepare them for the days that lie ahead. At this time in the life of these young people, help them by Thy Spirit to understand that Thou art willing to be their partner and companion in their work and in their journey through life. Remember them one by one and the homes they come from, and may they ever have a great faith to work and live by; for we ask in Jesus' Name. Amen.

PENTECOST SUNDAY

Scripture Lesson: Lev. 23:16-22.

Fifty days after Easter is Pentecost. It is also called the "Feast of Weeks" and "Feast of Harvest." The Feast of Pentecost was one of the three biggest events in the Jewish calendar. The other two were Passover (the time for this one also included the Feast of Unleavened Bread and First Fruits) and Tabernacles. During these three great events, all the men were to go to Jerusalem (Deut. 16:16). So following the Feast of First Fruits, they started counting. They counted the days and the weeks! They made minute preparations. Expectancy rose higher and higher. Excitement increased with the passing weeks and with the completion of preparations for this important event.

According to one authority, Palestine was divided into twenty-four districts, and a company came from each one. He says, "Each morning, while they were on the road to Jerusalem, their leader summoned them with the words, 'Come ye, let us go to Zion, and unto Jehovah our God' (Jer. 31:6), and they answered back, 'I was glad when they said unto me, Let us go into the house of the Lord' (Psalm 122:1)." The formations in which they marched are given thus: "First went one who played the pipe; then followed a sacrificial bullock, destined for a peace offering, his horns gilt and garlanded with olive branches; next came the multitude, some carrying baskets with the firstfruits, others singing psalms which many writers suppose to have been especially designed for that service, and hence to have been called 'The Songs of Ascent,' in our Authorized Version 'The Psalm of Degrees.' The poorer brought their gifts in a wicker basket, which afterwards belonged to the officiating priests; the richer brought theirs in baskets of silver or gold, which were given to the Temple Treasury, so they passed through the length and breadth of the land, everywhere waking the echoes of praise. What sights and sounds there must have been as the people from every district of Palestine headed for Jerusalem for this annual and historic event!"

That was Pentecost in Jewish history and New Testament Pentecost in type!

But what an event it was!

The descent of the Holy Spirit on the group waiting in the Upper Room in Jerusalem about nine o'clock on the morning of May 28th, A.D. 30, was a momentous event. About one hundred twenty men and women were filled with the Holy Spirit, and the Church was born. For the first three hundred years of the Christian Church, the name Pentecost indicated the entire period from Easter to Pentecost. The writings of Tertullian, Origen, Basil the Great and other sources indicate this early concept.

During this period the theaters were closed; games were suspended; the book of Acts was read in the liturgy; there was no feasting; prayer was offered standing (perhaps in commemoration of the descent of the Holy Spirit); and the Hallelujah was frequently sung.

After the third century, the observance of Pentecost became more restricted; and after the eighth century, this trend continued until the observance finally dropped to one day — Whitsunday. One of the saddest things in Christian history is that even the observance of Pentecost Sunday has continued to decline. The little emphasis that is placed on this significant event in the Christian Church is literally alarming. In most all religious circles, there is much ado about Easter and the forty days preceding it. Lent reaches a saturation point at Easter. This is the BIG DAY. The churches are crowded beyond capacity. In some cases two and three morning services are held. But, do you know what happened after Easter? The fifty days following Easter are some of the most historic days of the church. It was Easter, and what followed that substantiated what happened immediately preceding that day.

Easter is not the end. It is the beginning. This writer has pleaded for more emphasis on the fifty days following Easter. We continue to do so. This is one of the most significant periods of the church calendar, and the church needs to utilize them for its own good and for the evangelization of the world.

E. Stanley Jones, in his book entitled, *The Christ of Every Road,* copyrighted three decades ago, declares, "Imagine the early church with Pentecost eliminated." But today thousands of churches have done just that! The same author says, "The Church has shied away from Pentecost. There was a time when the Christian Church celebrated Whitsunday, the anniversary of the coming of the Spirit, more than it did Christmas, the anniversary of the coming of Christ." At Christmas they gave *gifts.* At Pentecost they gave *themselves.* Which cost more? He also said, "There is no doubt that the divine purpose was and is that Pentecost should be normal Christianity." Let's make it a perpetual movement and a continuing experience.

We are on this side of Easter, and we face Pentecost annually. The time to prepare for this event is now. It demands more emphasis than one day. It requires the utilization of all the fifty days leading up to this great event and more. It is worth all that we have and are. In recounting the method at arriving at the Feast of Pentecost, it is significantly recorded: "From the day you bring the sheaf of the wave offering, you shall COUNT FIFTY DAYS" (Lev. 23:13, Moffatt's translation).

THANKSGIVING

"And Isaac digged again the wells of water, which they had digged in the days of Abraham his father; . . . and he called their names after the names by which his father had called them" (Gen. 26:18).

In Old Testament times, a well of water was of the greatest value. In Bible lands it does not rain for nine full months out of the year. Whoever has a well has a fortune. The well was the meeting place for the travellers who crossed the plains. From it went streams of water to enrich the nearby land and make it blossom as a rose. Near to it travellers pitched their tents and sometimes took up their permanent abode. It was strength for the weak; it was refreshment for the weary; and in every respect a place of importance in the estimation of the people. A king who dug a well was made more famous than if he constructed a palace or shared in the erection of a pyramid.

Famous Wells in the Bible

Those wells dug by Abraham are of special importance. The lessons centering about them are capable of spiritual interpretation. This is evident from what we read in Isa. 12:2-3: "Behold, God is my salvation; I will trust and not be afraid: for the Lord Jehovah is my strength and my song; He also is become my salvation. Therefore with joy shall ye draw water out of the wells of salvation." The picture here given by the prophet is of the soul finding rest and refreshment in God, and its greatest joy in fellowship with man. It is sad to observe that today men have put God out of their lives. They are too busy seeking fortunes and happiness in things, such as jobs, clothes and material possessions. The soul separated from God is not only without salvation, but also without a song and without joy.

A New Testament Well

This one is the most wonderful of all. It is described in John 4:6, "Now Jacob's well was there. Jesus therefore, being wearied with his journey, sat thus on the well: and it was about the sixth hour." This well is eighty-four feet deep and is one of the few places in that area that contains fresh water. The writer drank from this well while there. It has fifteen of water. There are some sad stories in connection with this well. One has to do with Jacob's journey on his way to Bethel, and at this well-curb we have the warning which comes to us in the story of Jacob's heartbreaking experience. We are told in the story that when we start to walk with God, there must be no stopping at a half-way station, no compromise with the world. But there is a beautiful picture associated with this well. It was here that Jesus sat and forgave the Samaritan woman her sin and sent her on her way rejoicing and telling her story of the man who had not only changed her life but had told her all the things she ever did.

To me it is significant that this well has to do with the sad failure of Jacob's daughter Dinah and the same well has to do with the sin of another woman who was forgiven by the Lord Jesus Christ. This points up the difference between law and grace! The day the law was given three thousand were slain (Ex. 32:27-28). The day that grace began, three thousand were saved (Acts 2:41). Under the law, the sheep died for the shepherd. Under grace, the Shepherd died for the sheep (John 10:11). Under the law, the covenant was between God and man. Under grace, the covenant is between God the Father and God the Son, and we enter by faith into the finished work of Jesus. Under the law, a disobedient son was stoned with stones until he was dead (Ex. 21:15). Under grace, a disobedient son was mourned by his father, was loved in his wanderings, and when his father knew his son was coming home, was met with a kiss, a robe, a ring for his finger, and shoes for his feet. That father then called in his friends and neighbors to rejoice with him because his boy had been dead but was alive again.

Thanksgiving Day

It is a time for reunions, and in Old Testament times, they gathered about a well and had fellowship together. Now we gather about a fireside and rejoice that, as friends and loved ones, we are separated no more. Would it not be well on this Thanksgiving Day to dig a well which might mean a closer fellowship with God and His children and stir a stronger desire to please Him.

Joseph and Mary

A well was the place of farewell for this couple and the young child Jesus when they left Bethlehem at the conclusion of the feast of the Passover. They undoubtedly stopped at the well of Bethlehem, which is by the gate, and said farewell to their kindred and friends.

This well was always hallowed by sacred memories. When David was in the cave Addullam he cried out, "Oh that one would give me drink from the well which is in Bethlehem by the gate." Would it not be well on this Thanksgiving Day to dig a well, gather about it and record our vows that we will say good-by to a life of failure and set our faces toward a life of victory.

A Place of Refreshment

Jesus spoke of a well in this way. He said "He that drinketh of the water that I shall give him shall never thirst, it shall be in him a well of water" (John 4:14). Let us go back to the Old Book! It is water to a thirsty soul, it is food to the hungry, it is light to those in darkness, it is all that the spiritual nature demands. Some people have been drifting from the old wells, but without them life is worthless.

In olden times when Abraham dug his wells, he gave two of them very special names. The first was "Lahairoi" (Gen. 25:11). The name of this well signified "the well of him that liveth and seeth me." In these last days men in their sinful ways are living as if God knew nothing about them. I can think of no text of Scripture more strikingly useful today than this: "Thou God seest me." Professor James Orr once said, "God is shaking all things in heaven and earth, but the things that cannot be shaken remain." God remains, the Bible remains, Christ remains, sin and its ugliness are still with us. The Gospel which is God's provision for human sin and need remains.

The second well Abraham dug was named "Beersheba" (Gen. 22:19). This signifies "the well of the oath" or the covenant. These wells (after Abraham's death) were filled in by his enemies (Gen. 26:18).

It is easy to understand why Isaac's action suggests a message for Thanksgiving. Isaac's story is amazing. He is a child of promise, one of God's Old Testament miracles. Because of what Abraham was and what Jacob was, Isaac was not outstanding. He is between these two colorful characters and overshadowed by them. Isaac attempted to revive an old custom and dig some wells for himself. But note that the ones he dug were failures. In Gen. 26:20, we note that one of his wells was named "Esek" and that means strife. In Gen. 26:21 the other was named "Sitnah" and that means hatred. We might as well learn we cannot improve on God's plans for saving souls and operating His work. The old blue-print is better than the new experiment.

Let's dig again the wells of our fathers, and let us first have better homes. When fathers are too busy and mothers too worldly, children suffer. When fathers are priests of their households and mothers are saints, the home is like heaven. Better homes and better churches make better living. Automobiles are carrying people away from home and church on the Lord's day. The golf course is absorbing men's energy on Sunday and doing harm. The Lord's day must be observed and not be a holiday or a fun day.

Another well should be mentioned. Isa. 55:1, "Lo, every one that thirsteth, come ye to the waters, and he that hath no money; come ye, buy, and eat; yea, come, buy wine and milk without money and without price." The water of life is made possible for all who are athirst. Jesus said, "I am Alpha and Omega, the beginning and the end. I will give unto him that is athirst of the fountain of the water of life freely." The enemies of the Cross have tried to fill this well, too! This Thanksgiving is a fitting season to open wide the old wells again.

CHRISTMAS

"For unto us a child is born, unto us a son is given: and the government shall be upon his shoulder: and his name shall be called Wonderful, Counselor, the mighty God, the everlasting Father, the Prince of Peace" (Isa. 9:6).

Only a short while from now, another Christmas will be but a memory. A few moments more to linger in the colorful radiance of the Christmas tree, a few moments more to blend our hearts and voices in Christmas melodies, a few moments more to enjoy the happiness that comes to our united family circles on Christmas, and this day of days will be released from our grasp and will give way to the tomorrow. Then the spell of Christmas will be broken for many, its luster dimmed and its message forgotten.

But Christmas is too magnificent to be confined to one solitary, fleeting day. This Christ of Christmas is a gift that brings perpetual happiness both here and hereafter. If you have never permitted the star of faith to guide you to Bethlehem, I urge you now to join the lowly shepherds and follow them to the Christ child and immortalize this Christmas by receiving Him into the "inn" of your heart.

Seven hundred years before the angels aroused these drowsy shepherds, Isaiah of the Old Testament predicted His birth and gave to Him the dynamic titles contained in our text. He identifies Him by five glorious names.

Wonderful

Isiah calls the Christchild first of all "Wonderful." This title in the original is "The Miracle." Here let us stop and breathe a word of thankful prayer that He is a miracle and beyond human reason and understanding. He is the mystery of God becoming incarnate as the Son of Man. Is it any wonder that unbelieving man cries out, "How can these things be?" The religion of Jesus is based upon a miracle. True, it is not man's way of working, but it is God's way. Let those who hear the Christmas Gospel only believe and kneel before the Wonder of the Ages, and like Christian-minded Magi, offer Him the pure gold of faith, the fragrant frankincense of hope and the myrrh of love.

This Christ child is the supreme miracle in the history of all lands and ages, and I wish to declare that this Babe in the manger is the super solution to the universal problem of sin. The Bible gives its warning indictment, "all have sinned." It points the finger of accusation at you, "Thou art the man," but Christmas points us to the name given Him before His birth in this manner, "Thou shalt call his name Jesus for he shall save his people from their sins." There is no sin too great, no offense too vile, no wrong too oppressive to be removed completely for all time by His priceless birth and death on the cross.

Counselor

The past year may have brought you a long series of disappointments. You may have gone on year after year with a good deal of confidence in your money, brain power and social power, but this house of cards may have been blown over, and you may be looking for some one to lift you out of your bewilderment. You can find a Counselor today in Bethlehem. He is concerned first and foremost, not with your money or social prestige, but with that soul that lives on after the trinkets of men crumble into dust. Here is the faithful Counselor telling us in Matt. 6:33, "Seek ye first the kingdom of God and his righteousness," that is, get right with God. Remove the barrier that separates you from God and keeps you from the happiness which makes life worth living. When you say, "How can I remove the sin from my life?" the Wonderful Counselor, this Christ, tells us, "I am the way, the truth, and the life." Believe in Him. His counsel has never failed. Look above your sin and difficulties to the Babe of Bethlehem's manger and believe Him when He calls out to you, "Come unto me all ye that labor and are heavy laden and I will give you rest" (Matt. 11:28).

The Mighty God

The third name of this wonder child is "The Mighty God." Here we have the real, essential Christ of Christmas; the Christ who from the lowly beginning at Bethlehem until the bitter, heartbreaking end at Calvary, proved to be and was declared to be, "God manifest in the flesh" (I Tim. 3:16). The prophet Isaiah in foretelling His birth (7:14) calls Him "Immanuel," meaning *God with us.* What for? To turn the night of sin and sorrow into radiant day. God is with us in the happiness of our homes, in the stern realities of every day life. God is with us in the trials and temptations that bear down upon one. God is with us as the unfailing light to guide us, Friend to uphold us, and Saviour now and forevermore.

Everlasting Father

The fourth name for this helpless infant is "The Everlasting Father." Let us linger for a moment on these two names of majestic meaning, "Everlasting" and "Father." Throughout man's long existence, he has strained for something firm and enduring, but his greatest achievements rise today and fade tomorrow. They are here one day and gone the next. But now I want you to look with me at this Pillar of the Ages – a changeless Christ for a changing world. "He is the same yesterday, today and forever" (Heb. 13:8). He is "King of Kings" and "Lord of Lords" and has made a peace treaty between heaven and earth that has been signed and sealed by His blood on the cross.

Prince of Peace

Some of you are still at war with God, still allied with the forces of sin. Let me urge you to come and accept peace for the soul, not as the world gives, but the peace that Christ, our Shiloh, offers to all. You will never know the joy of life until this peace is pronounced upon your sin-free soul. Only this step will make Christmas be to you what it should be – the birthday of Christ, the Prince of Peace, not only in Bethlehem, but also in your soul.

MUSIC APPRECIATION SUNDAY

"To be able to make music and sing is a divine gift from God." Although that ability is not always to be divinely used, nevertheless it is divinely given. It has always held a high place in worship and evangelism. It has been and will always be man's common and effective method of expressing his love, devotion, and praise to God. When used and presented for God's glory, whether in worship or routing the enemy, it will always find its mark. In the song of Moses we find praises ringing out to God for His deliverance. The Psalms proclaim the greatness of God, while in 2 Chronicles 20, we find music as a weapon destroying the enemy. While surrounded by their enemy, Jehoshaphat, instead of selecting men to bear arms, appointed singers, a choir, and equipped them with a song book. As they were approaching the enemy they were singing, and the Lord set ambushments against them, and everyone helped destroy the other (2 Chron. 20:23). All this was accomplished through song.

Whatever song we sing or wherever we sing, there must be harmony between audible and inward voice. When these two are blended together, there will be results. Spiritual results are not always brought about by the best singers, but rather by those who blend these two voices together. Often this is done by an old, grey-haired mother whose voice is no longer clear and strong, but the audible is in perfect harmony with the inward spirit and the song finds its mark. These will not be remembered as singers, but their song will leave a lasting impression on those who hear it.

A Director of Music should have some spiritual qualifications. The same ones would apply to any singer or musician, but we have the director in mind, since so much rests upon him for the spiritual life of the service. First of all, he must be sensitive to the leadership of the Holy Spirit. Unless he prays and seeks the counsel of God in selecting his songs and musical program, it is probable that he will be of little value to the spirituality of the service. Often he becomes a detriment instead of an asset. One testimony, one prayer, or any other event can and often does change the result of the service. Unless the director of music is "prayed up" and in touch with God, the meeting could easily end at this crucial point in shipwreck. On the other hand, if he is "prayed up" and in touch with God, he will direct the chorus or singing in a manner that is in harmony with the type of spirit prevailing. He sets the heartbeat for the service. He can open the door for the work of the Holy Ghost, or he can close Him out.

The result of the service from first to last depends largely upon the director of music. The effectiveness of a testimony meeting, healing service, altar or preaching service, is supported largely by music and song. Singing in evangelism must be associated with worship and praise. Too often singers, and sometimes ministers, have regarded it as only a part of the form of service. The most common of all mistakes is associating it with entertainment. Often more interest is given to "beautifying" the song than in seeking God's anointing upon it.

Most certainly singers should train their voices and constantly endeavor to improve their wonderful God-given talent. Let us keep in mind, however, that it will avail little unless God places His approval upon it, and it is sung under the anointing of the Holy Ghost. God does not consider the quality; He takes note of the spirit in which it is sung.

Singing should entertain, but when it stops with entertainment, it is sadly missing its mark. It was never given and ordained of God to end with entertainment, but to motivate praise and worship. Some acquaintances of mine have driven hundreds of miles to be entertained by what is called a "Battle of Songs". In my humble opinion this is nothing but a sanctified contest of voices and songs. This is as much out of place as a "Battle of Sermons" or a "Battle of Testimonies." Music was meant to have a more sacred meaning than that.

Christianity is a singing religion. This does not mean you have to be a singer to have salvation; it does mean that if you have heartfelt salvation, there will be a song in your heart.

I have seen some people who could put much energy and enthusiasm into a song and get very little harmony out of it, but their song would inspire others to worship. This is where early-day Methodist people got their reputations as singers.

Paul said, "Whatsover ye do, do it heartily, as unto the Lord." They sang unto the Lord and not unto man, and whole communities were stirred for God through their singing. Theirs wasn't always the best and the most beautiful, but it inspired and moved people to action because it was sung unto the Lord. It is important that we remember this.

This writer knows singers who are not the best singers by any means, yet God has honored and rewarded their efforts because they used their talents unto God. By their singing they have moved people to God who had resisted invitations in sermons during their entire lives. These singers pray and seek God for the right song as much as a minister seeks God for the right sermon. These people carry an anointing in their ministry of music and song. I urge our musicians and singers, and especially the directors of music, to put music and songs in their proper place. Seek God's will and season the songs with prayer.

While it is true Christianity is a singing religion, and we know most of its use in worship and devotion, music and singing is found at the heart of most all other religions of the world. It is true they do not all use the same type of music in connection with worship. The primitive peoples of ancient times had their tom-toms, gongs, and bells; the Greeks, their panpipes, and the Israelites their harps, trumpets, cymbals, flutes, drums, and other instruments.

Hebrew worship consisted principally of singing, accompanied by instruments, together with sacrifices and other rites prescribed by the Mosaic law. The book of Psalms was the hymn book of these people. This makes the book of Psalms the oldest hymn book in existence, and it was used for many centuries, even down to New Testament times. The choirs used in connection with the temple worship were extremely large and world famous. During the days of David, in anticipation of the building of the temple, there were 288 singers, divided into 24 groups (1 Chronicles 25:1-31). During the days of Nehemiah, 245 are mentioned (Nehemiah 7:67).

As part of the observance of the Passover, it was a custom for them to sing portions of the Psalms including one hundred fifteen to one hundred eighteen. It is thought by certain Jewish authorities that these are the Psalms Jesus and His disciples sang in the upper room before crossing to the garden of Gethsemane (Matt. 26:30). The Psalms headed "Songs of Degrees," and "Songs of Ascent," were used by the pilgrims as they came and went to Jerusalem at the times of the three great feasts; namely, Pentecost, the Passover, and the Feast of Tabernacles (Deut. 16:16).

Its Place in the New Testament. It is soul enriching just to read of the place music and singing had in the first century church. Scriptures refer to "songs and hymns and spiritual songs" (Ephesians 5:18, 19 and Colossians 3:16), as well as to hymns sung privately, such as Paul and Silas sang while confined in the Philippian jail (Acts 16:25).

The singing of hymns tends to draw the soul away from the cares of life and center it on God. Singing together makes us forget the spiritual isolation in which most of us live the greater part of the time. It has a unifying effect. Congratulations to our choirs for their beautiful numbers; they have lifted us up and made spiritual things real and precious.

Another style was originated for liturgical services, arranged for use in the great cathedrals by highly trained choirs, rather than by the people in the pews. The first use of the organ is not known, but it was certainly in use before the fourth century. The early idea of compressing air by water was soon replaced by the use of the bellows, but for centuries the wind supply was clumsy and inefficient. As late as A.D. 950 it is recorded that seventy men acted as blowers in the Winchester Cathedral. The pipes which ranged in number from eight to twenty-six in the fourth century, had been increased to four hundred in the tenth.

After the beginning of the Protestant Reformation in 1517, music came back to the people again and was made an auxiliary to worship. Hymns immediately began to be written and people were encouraged to join in congregational singing. Luther, the great Reformer said, "The Lord speaks to us through His holy Word, and we, in turn, speak to Him in prayer and songs of praise." Luther himself wrote many hymns, the greatest of which is "A Mighty Fortress Is Our God." The Wesleyan Revival likewise brought many new hymns, with Isaac Watts as the great hymn writer of the eighteenth century.

In Germany the advance of church music, both vocal and instrumental, came to a climax in Bach, a devout churchman, who wrote approximately three hundred cantatas as well as other great music. Handel wrote "The Messiah," which is an earnest expression of his convictions and feelings. Mozart composed much church music, which included a number of cantatas. These men regarded their musical gifts as divinely given, and their productions will go on enriching the worship of the church till Jesus comes.

It was while these great composers were busy in Europe, that the earliest American compositions made their appearance. Francis Hopkinson and James Lyon were both composing as early as 1759, and after 1770, there were many compositions of sacred music in New England by William Billings, Andrew Law, and Daniel Read. Since that time there have been literally hundreds of hymn writers in America, and we have been richly blessed by their productions.

Pliny, the historian, gave a report to the Roman Emperor of how the second century Christians sang in Bithynia, in this manner: "The Christians affirmed that it was their custom to meet on a stated day before sunrise, and sing a hymn to Christ; that they bound themselves by an oath never to commit any crime, but to abstain from adultery, theft, never to break their word, nor to deny a trust when summoned to deliver it; after which they would separate and then reassemble for the purpose of eating in common a harmless meal" (Pliny, Epist. X:96).

The new faith naturally called for new hymns, the earliest we possess being written by Clement of Alexandria, who died about A.D.

220. Chrysostom (347-407), in commenting on the effect of music on people, said, "Wheresoever ungodly songs are sung, there will be devils gathered together; and wheresoever spiritual songs are sung, there will the grace of the Spirit fly, and sanctify both mouth and soul. I say these things not only that ye yourselves may give praise, but that ye may teach both your wives and children to sing such songs when engaged at the loom, or in other labors, but especially at meat."

Augustine (354-430) tells the effect that the singing of Christian hymns had on him at the time of his baptism: "Oh, how freely was I made to weep by these hymns and spiritual songs; transported by the voices of the congregation sweetly singing. The melody of their voices filled my ear, and divine truth was poured into my heart. Then burned the sacred flame of devotion in my soul, and gushing tears flowed from my eyes, as well they might."

As the church changed from a simple New Testament organization to an ecclesiastical system dominated by Rome during the Middle Ages, singing was taken away from the people and became a function of the clergy; the words were put in Latin.

BIBLE SUNDAY

"I will not forget thy Word" (Psa. 119:16).

A noted unbeliever, in arrogance, said, "It took twelve men to establish Christianity. I will show the world that one man can pull it to pieces. In one hundred years the Bible will become obsolete and relegated to the shelves of the forgotten." The time is more than up. In spite of scoffers that have come and gone, there is a greater demand for the Bible today than at any time in history.

Our printing presses turn out an average of six hundred Bibles an hour, and fifteen thousand a day. It has happened at certain times that nine tons of Bibles have been printed in twenty-eight different languages in a single day. The twenty-one "best-sellers" have had a combined sale of sixty-five million copies, whereas, the Bible sales have reached two billion copies. This enormous production proves the Scriptures to be the light of men. Even in times like these we can find in the Bible message the way out and the way UP!

Why do men not read the Bible? Some do not read it because there is so much else to read. Others think that scientists have proved the Bible account of creation as given in the book of Genesis wrong in favor of the theory of evolution. But before we say we are not impressed with the behavior of men like Noah, Isaac, and Jacob; and that we are bored by the ceremonials of Leviticus and Chronicles; and conclude by asking if Paul was not trying to start a new religion; let's see Jesus' estimate of the Holy Scriptures. He says in Matt. 5:17, 18, "Think not that I am come to destroy the law [writings of Moses and the prophets] or the prophets: I am not come to destroy, but to fulfill. For verily I say unto you, Till heaven and earth pass, one jot or one tittle shall in no wise pass from the law, till all be fulfilled." The Old Testament Scriptures have the full approval of the Saviour. Many have forgotten His Word because of listening to the dirt and trash of our time. On this day of Universal Bible observance let us go back and listen again to the Voice from Sinai, the music of Psalms, the messages of Isaiah and Amos, the Sermon on the Mount, and the preaching of the Apostles.

The Bible was never intended to become a memory! To many people it is just that! Today they are looking into the Ouija board instead of the Bible for an answer to the fundamental problems of life. Yes, they still possess Bibles but they have ceased to use them. The sight of them recalls the memory of days gone by. They remember when these Bibles were given them. They read them at that time. They were young then. But now they are grown up men and women and their Bibles have been laid aside. The hour has struck for us to get our Bibles back!

We have celebrated the three hundredth anniversary of the landing of the Pilgrims. Do not forget it was the Bible that made the men of the "Mayflower" what they were. It was a lamp to their feet and a light to their path. The Pilgrims were a people of that Book. Their hopes of liberty hung upon their Bibles. On it our Commonwealth has been built. They believed that the Bible spoke with authority, and that the "Thus saith the Lord" was a word to be obeyed. We can profit from the example of the Pilgrims and no better way can be found to honor their memory than by accepting their reverence for the Book.

The Bible is far out in front in circulation. It is a "best-seller" and remains, year in and year out, in a class to itself. Many new books come on the market each year, but none ever crowds the Bible aside. It is the only book competition never disturbs. The average Bible sales are forty thousand a day. There is only one solid reason why this is so. Men feel they want and need a message from God; therefore, they turn to His Book to get it.

In hours of strain, in any solemn hour of life, men instinctively turn to the Bible. For instance, when the world fares ill, the Bible comes into its own. When business is bad, Bible business is good. This was graphically true in the South during the Civil War. As the distress and grief of 1862 came home to every plantation in the South, when the great outside world turned its back on them, then the Bible became precious to the people and began to win its way back. This experience left an imprint on that and succeeding generations. For since 1865, the South, composed of English stock, has had more reverence for the written Word of God than any other portion of the country.

During wars the sale of Bibles and Testaments reached its highest figures. When we were in the old war, one Bible House reported the sale of a million copies in a single year. It is true that many people, old and young, forget God's Word while the sun of health and prosperity is shining, but let woe overtake them, sickness lay them low and they turn to the Bible like a child to its mother. Look at a map of the world. Look at Bible Lands, and lands that do not have the Bible. The differences between them is as great as darkness is from light, life from death, and stagnation from progress.

The Bible is the book that has done most for the world! Sir Walter Scott was not a very religious man. But when he came to die he said, "There is but one book. Read to me the Bible." John Ruskin has gone on record as saying that the learning of the Bible by heart as a boy did more for him than all the rest of his education. Abraham Lincoln built up his education on the Bible, which was one of the few books he had as a boy. When Henry Stanley was a boy, his foster parents put him in a workhouse where he was whipped if he mispronounced an Old Testament name. Years later when he was in darkest Africa, he declared he would gladly go through it all again for what the Bible did for him while he was alone in that wilderness. When Theodore Roosevelt chose a half dozen books to take with him to Africa, one was the Bible.

But the roll call would not be complete without mentioning the saints and heroes we have known in our homes and communities. It was the Bible that made them what they were. Suzanna Wesley, the mother of John and Charles the founders of Methodism, had a family of eighteen children, yet she did not forget God's Word, and was considered one of the best informed persons of her day on the Bible.

It contains a message so personal that each one who truly reads it, feels that it was written just for him; it just fits his own case; it just matches his own need; it gives just the help and just the light his emergency requires. Coleridge once said, "I know the Bible is inspired, because it inspires me." But the point is, it inspires every one.

One of the wonders of the Bible is that it never grows old; it never passes out of date. It has an original value and message for every age, and a secret message for the secret needs of each soul. Realize this and the Bible will have a new meaning for you. The Bible does not argue. It never argues. It speaks with authority that carries comfort and conviction. It tells us that God loves us. That faith in Him saves our souls. That forgiveness is offered us "without money and without price." That His mercy is boundless and covers the lost of all the earth.

TEMPERANCE SUNDAY

"Nor drunkards" (Gal. 5:21).

"Wine is a mocker, strong drink is raging, and whosoever is deceived thereby is not wise" (Prov. 20:1).

"Look not thou upon the wine when it is red, when it giveth his color in the cup, when it moveth itself aright. At last it biteth like a serpent, and stingeth like an adder" (Prov. 23:31-32).

"Nor thieves, nor covetous, nor drunkards, nor revilers, nor extortioners, shall inherit the kingdom of God" (1 Cor. 6:10).

It is amazing that in Rev. 12 and 20, the devil is called a "serpent." In Proverbs wine is said to "move in the cup and bite like a serpent." Rev. 20:10 says "the devil was cast into the lake of fire" and Paul tells us in 1 Cor. 6:10 the "drunkard" does not inherit the kingdom of God. Both are called serpents, and both land in hell.

There are six million people in our country right now whose lives will be shortened because of excessive drinking.

When General Marshall was asked what was America's greatest threat, he replied, "cocktail bars." It is estimated by those in the "know" that this country spends enough on liquor in one year to give every family $236.00 as an outright gift.

We usually speak of foreign countries as being lovers of intoxicating drinks, but this year we spent twice as much as the German people did for drink.

Dr. Chappell studied 29,000 pupils in high schools, and the survey revealed 90 per cent of the pupils drank and that this drinking began in some cases before the child was 11 years old. It was found that 93 per cent of the homes were stocked with liquor.

Women greatest offenders. Women do most of the buying for the home. Satan has somehow included beer on the grocery list, and 55 per cent of the beer sold in America is sold at the grocery store to the housewives. You will observe that this is on a national scale. We are sowing drink on every corner, and we will reap a nation of drunkards, and God's judgments will certainly fall.

We look at Babylon in Dan. 5 and see what happened when sacred vessels were turned into liquor glasses. In modern times we have heard of drunkenness in foreign lands. We saw Mussolini's and Hitler's empires defy God and fall in the dust. We tell ourselves it can't happen here, but let's listen to Jesus when He said, "Except ye repent, ye shall all likewise perish" (Luke 13:3).

One of the worst things Satan has used against our nation is the bars, saloons, cafes, drug stores and restaurants stocked with liquor across our land.

This concerns Christians. We who believe in living by the Bible should note what it says. Gen. 9:20 to 26 records the drunkenness of Noah. Gen. 19:30 to 38 tells of Lot's backsliding and sin caused by drunkenness. In Judges 13:4, the mother of Samson was told to beware of strong drink. I Kings 16:9 tells how a king died in drunkenness. In I Kings 20:16 an army fails and is defeated through drink. These are only a few references that show the wickedness of this awful sin.

If you are a child of God, you should have no time for anything that will ruin another man's soul. This thing of saying, "Hallelujah, 'tis done, I believe on the Son," and then going down the alley and drinking with the devil's goats — you are just as bad as they are. The Bible calls for the child of God to come out and be separate and touch not the unclean thing (2 Cor. 6:17). If only more Christians would rise up and shake off the devil's fleas and would realize the liquor business has the devil's power behind it, we would have a mighty revival that would rock this nation. It's a deceiver because it tells you you're rich when you don't have a penny, tells you you don't have a pain when you are dying with cancer, and last but not least, it tells you everything is all right while your poor deceived soul is in the hands of the devil on the road to an eternal hell. But God gives a new heart. He will give the drunkard a new one. There is hope for any drunkard the same as there is for any sinner. Drunkenness is one of the many sins that keep people out of heaven. I do not mean to tell you that if you are a drunkard and quit drinking, that will take you to heaven. If you were to quit drinking by your own will power, the devil would soon involve you in other sin because you were born with a wicked nature that knows nothing but rebellion against God.

The only answer is the *New Birth*. To be born all over again, with a new heart, a new mind, a whole new nature in harmony with God. This will happen when you realize how sinful you have been and accept Jesus as your Saviour. God's Word tells us we have sinned (Rom. 3:23). He plainly tells us Jesus bore our sins in His body on the tree (1 Pet. 2:24). This same Jesus rose from the dead and today calls for all those who are lost in sin to come to Him.